Lecture Notes in Computer Science 5963

Commenced Publication in 1973
Founding and Former Series Editors:
Gerhard Goos, Juris Hartmanis, and Jan van Leeuwen

David England   Philippe Palanque
Jean Vanderdonckt   Peter J. Wild (Eds.)

Task Models and Diagrams for User Interface Design

8th International Workshop, TAMODIA 2009
Brussels, Belgium, September 23-25, 2009
Revised Selected Papers

 Springer

Volume Editors

David England
Liverpool John Moores University
School of Computing and Mathematical Sciences
Byrom Street, Liverpool, L3 3AF, UK
E-mail: d.england@ljmu.ac.uk

Philippe Palanque
University Paul Sabatier, Institute of Research in Informatics of Toulouse (IRIT)
118 Route de Narbonne, 31062 Toulouse Cedex 9, France
E-mail: palanque@irit.fr

Jean Vanderdonckt
Université Catholique de Louvain
Place des Doyens 1, 1348 Louvain-La-Neuve, Belgium
E-mail: jean.vanderdonckt@uclouvain.be

Peter J. Wild
University of Cambridge, Institute for Manufacturing
17 Charles Babbage Road, Cambridge, CB3 0FS, UK
E-mail: peter.j.wild@gmail.com

Library of Congress Control Number: 2009943841

CR Subject Classification (1998): H.5, D.2, I.3.6, I.3.7, K.4, K.8

LNCS Sublibrary: SL 2 – Programming and Software Engineering

ISSN   0302-9743
ISBN-10   3-642-11796-1 Springer Berlin Heidelberg New York
ISBN-13   978-3-642-11796-1 Springer Berlin Heidelberg New York

Typesetting: Camera-ready by author, data conversion by Scientific Publishing Services, Chennai, India
Printed on acid-free paper   SPIN: 12985890   06/3180   5 4 3 2 1 0

Foreword

TAMODIA 2009 was the 8th International Workshop in the series looking at TAsk MOdels and DIAgrams for User Interface Development. Over the years the submissions have looked at a variety of perspectives for modeling and annotating the user interface development process. The eighth workshop continued that approach and was combined with the IFIP Working Conference on Human Error, Safety and Systems Development, HESSD 2009. There is an obvious synergy between the two workshops, as a rigorous, engineering approach to user interface development can help in the prevention of human error and the maintenance of safety in critical interactive systems.

The 12 papers presented here take a variety of approaches and cover different domains of the application of task modeling. We begin with higher-level perspectives on business processes that enable us to drive user interface development. Aspects of the general design process are also considered and applied to service-oriented and augmented reality interaction. Formal methods are also investigated for more rigorous development. Model-driven development is also recognized for its contribution to high-level interface design, and continuing the software engineering theme, approaches based on UML are presented.

Sousa et al. propose a model-driven approach to linking business processes with user interface models. Their approach is demonstrated in the context of a large financial institution and they show how the alignment between UI models and business can be managed, taking advantage of the traceability provided by model-driven design. Neubauer et al. also consider a flow-oriented modeling of business processes as a more open approach to capturing the dynamics of process modeling and understanding. Fritscher and Pigneur consider a more creative approach to business modeling with their ontology canvas that aims to provide a template for the interactive modeling of business processes very early in the development life cycle.

Looking at the design process itself, Media et al. take a service-oriented approach to supporting user interface developers at the operational, organizational and intentional levels of design abstraction. Octavia et al. look at the context of virtual and augmented reality environments and consider how adaption can be supported in design, where the adaptations of the interface are driven by context changes. Moving on to more formal considerations of development, Randles et al. consider the situation calculus as the basis for interaction modeling. They investigate their proposal for the situation calculus in the context of a complex medical system and also draw on lessons from autonomic computing in providing system self-management. Caffiau et al. consider current limitations in the description of objects in user interface specification. They examine the K-MADe tool and consider modifications that balance the needs of free expression by developers with the need for rigorous description of the objects.

Though model-driven development has been touched on earlier, it is considered in more depth by our next set of contributions. Van den Bergh et al. consider an approach where the task model is the central control point for the adaptation of the interface development. They consider not just synchronization at design-time but also the configuration of user interface models and application logic. Fleischmann et al. discuss subject-oriented business process management, which ensures coherence between modeling and execution through focusing on the communication flow among process participants (subjects) in the course of work-task accomplishment. They use Hoares CSP as the basis for model coherence checking. Martinez-Ruiz et al. consider the requirements for modeling for zoomable, multimedia interfaces. They propose weighted task hierarchies as a method for overcoming some of the complexities of modeling more complex interfaces.

In our final selection of papers the role of UML is examined. Nunes describes an approach to adapt the use-case point estimation method to fit the requirements of agile development of interactive software. The paper aims to further close the gap between HCI and software engineering, particularly at the earliest stages of development. Finally, Tran et al. present an agent-based framework to support automatic database user interface design and code generation where agents link the task model, context model and domain model of the system.

These 12 papers represent 50% of those submitted. Each paper was reviewed by three members of the Program Committee and their judgments were then reviewed by the Co-chairs. We trust the reader will find the papers useful in their work. This is the final TAMODIA event. In future it will be part of the ACM Symposium on Engineering Interactive Computer Systems.

We acknowledge the work of the reviewers in reviewing and giving feedback to the authors to improve their submissions. We thank the organizers of HESSD for cohosting TAMODIA 2009: Jean Vanderdonckt, Philippe Palanque and Marco Winckler. We would also like to thank Jean Vanderdonckt and his colleagues at UC Louvain for their hospitality and help in organizing activities during the workshops.

November 2009   David England
                                                          Peter J. Wild

Organization

General Chair

Peter J. Wild   University of Cambridge, UK

Program Chair

David England   Liverpool John Moores University, UK

Local Organization Chair

Jean Vanderdonckt   Université catholique de Louvain, Belgium

Proceedings Editor & Website

Marco Winckler   University Paul Sabatier, France

Program Committee

B. Bomsdorf	University of Applied Sciences Fulda, Germany
G. Calvary	IMAG, France
K. Coninx	University of Hasselt, Belgium
M.F. Costabile	University of Bari, Italy
A. Dittmar	University of Rostock, Germany
P. Forbrig	University of Rostock, Germany
E. Furtado	University of Fortaleza, Brazil
J. Karat	IBM, USA
M. Lozano	University of Castilla-La Mancha, Spain
K. Luyten	University of Hasselt, Belgium
M. Massink	Consiglio Nazionale delle Ricerche, Italy
N. Nunes	University of Madeira, Portugal
P. Palanque	University Paul Sabatier (Toulouse 3), France
F. Paternò	Consiglio Nazionale delle Ricerche, Italy
C. Pribeanu	National Institute for R&D in Informatics, Romania
C. Santoro	Consiglio Nazionale delle Ricerche, Italy
C. Sas	University of Lancaster, UK
K. Schneider	University of Saskatchewan, Canada
M. Sikorski	Gdansk University of Technology, Poland

P. Slavík   Czech Technical University in Prague,
                           Czech Republic
C. Stephanidis   University of Crete, Greece
H. Traetteberg   Norwegian University of Science and
                           Technology, Norway
J. Vanderdonckt   Catholic University of Louvain, Belgium
G. van der Veer   VU University Amersterdam,
                           The Netherlands
M. Winckler   University Paul Sabatier (Toulouse 3), France

Sponsoring Institutions

IHCS: Interacting Humans with Computing Systems, University Paul Sabatier
Université catholique de Louvain Belgian Laboratory of Computer-Human
    Interaction (BCHI)
Liverpool John Moores University
Brunel University
University of Cambridge
British Human-Computer Interaction Group

Table of Contents

Task Models and UML

A Rule-Based Approach for Model Management in a User Interface – Business Alignment Framework

Kenia Sousa, Hildeberto Mendonça, and Jean Vanderdonckt

Université catholique de Louvain, Louvain School of Management,
Place des Doyens, 1, 1348 Louvain-la-Neuve, Belgium
{kenia.sousa,hildeberto.mendonca,
jean.vanderdonckt}@uclouvain.be

Abstract. When organizations change Business Processes (BP) aiming for improvements, such changes normally impact on systems' User Interfaces (UI), which represent a tangible resource for communication with customers, suppliers, partners, or investors; thus a source of competitive advantage and differentiation. To manage the link between UIs and BPs, we propose a framework that classifies the core elements and the operations performed on them, represented through rules that are used to support impact analysis. This solution has been analyzed in a large bank-insurance organization, which has enabled the proposal of an innovative strategy that integrates researches on interaction design and business process management with implications on practical scenarios of result-driven organizations.

Keywords: Business Process Modeling, Model Driven Engineering, Interaction Design, User Interface Markup Language.

1 Introduction

In the competitive market, organizations are now, more than ever, struggling to innovate in order to provide added value to customers through their services and products. To corroborate this, the 2007 Aberdeen Report states that 46% of over 3,600 surveyed enterprises are managing changes to improve BPs with an additional 39% planning to do the same [1]. BPs enable innovation because they are tangible representations of strategic decisions translated into executable operations. Since BPs are executed in practice through enterprise systems they must be aligned to enable organizations to execute changes with flexibility.

However, it is no longer only system processing time that is pivotal for large organizations to improve their services for customers. A consultant from the Center of Excellence in Process-Efficient Technology has presented results of a study, conducted with 29 companies that had their enterprise systems developed aligning business processes with UIs and 23 companies with systems developed using traditional approaches. It has shown that the alignment primarily contributed to 100 to 200 percent user productivity gains [10].

Several recent strategies to align BPs with Information Technology (IT) and model-driven UI development address impacts on IT infra-structure and on the functional core

D. England et al. (Eds.): TAMODIA 2009, LNCS 5963, pp. 1–14, 2010.
© Springer-Verlag Berlin Heidelberg 2010

with solutions that automate the generation of systems to provide alignment. On the other hand, there are several organizations that already have their BPs and systems and cannot afford to re-develop their solutions with new technologies, but need to analyze impact of changes on their BPs and systems. Therefore, we have innovated by aligning IT with BPs through UIs, originally calling the term *UI-Business Alignment*, which analyzes impact of changes independent of the way BPs are structured and modeled, and how UIs are designed and developed. Here, the concept of *alignment* [9] addresses the *fit* between the external business arena and the internal structure and the *integration* of BP with UIs by considering how choices made on UIs impact those on the business domain and vice-versa.

One of the main innovative aspects of UI-Business alignment is that it focuses on business process actors, who are also system users, instead of uniquely on the systems, which has been extensively done so far. Our framework identifies impacts in terms of UIs that are understood by anyone who interacts with systems. On the other hand, traditional IT-Business alignment strategies present impact analysis in terms of system architecture, such as web services or classes, which are understood only by specialized professionals (e.g. system analysts, software architects).

This paper presents the main concepts of the models involved in the UI-Business Alignment (section 2). These concepts are the core elements of the rules that represent the foundation to maintain the mappings between the models (section 3). We present related works (section 4) and conclude with a summary and future work (section 5).

2 Model-Driven Approach for Traceability

The UI-Business alignment framework is composed of a methodology that has core actions to be performed by stakeholders who need to make sure that what is specified in BPs are executed by system end-users and what is suggested by users is considered in the business context. Among these actions, the traceability is possible by associating BPs with users' tasks, associating users' tasks with UIs, simulating impact of changes in any of these models, etc. This methodology can be combined with other corporate methods and processes, such as software development processes, HCI methods, process improvement methodologies, IT-Business alignment strategies, etc.

The UI-Business alignment framework adopts a model-driven approach for UI design, in which BPs, task models and UI models are mapped. We support the association of task models with UI models through relevant model-driven UI design works. Mapping the UI models is supported by UsiXML [21], a UI definition language that represents models in a structured form and supports the flexibility necessary for defining model-driven UIs; and by the Cameleon Reference Framework [7], extended with business process modeling. Following, we explain the link between these models that form the foundation for the proposed traceability strategy.

2.1 Business Process Models and Task Models

BP is a structured set of activities, performed by organizations' stakeholders, designed to produce a specific output for a particular customer or market [8]. Task models describe how tasks can be performed to reach users' goals when using systems. Task models are designed in a task hierarchical structure that contains different levels of abstraction, which starts with tasks in the highest level that are further decomposed in sub-tasks in the intermediary levels until the lowest level.

BP could not be directly associated to UIs because they represent the business context and some of their characteristics make them a limited representation for UI design, namely: 1) concepts in BPs do not consider automation in itself. The one responsible for applying the process decides what should be automated, not exactly how the activity is performed. 2) BPs do not encompass tasks intrinsic to user interaction (e.g. cancel, save temporarily, undo). 3) In most cases, the BP is not detailed enough to describe individual behavior and even when it is, the sequence of activities may not represent the user behavior, strongly influenced by the context of use. However, the BP structure is suitably similar to the hierarchical structure in task models, which influenced the use of task models as a bridge between BP and UIs.

2.2   Task Models and UI Models

To define user interaction, user tasks contain essential information to conceive UIs, a means by which users interact with the system. There are approaches that focus on mapping task and UI models to generate UIs. Paternò & Santoro [14] specify the relationships between task model and AUI, and between the AUI and its implementation. Brown et al. [6] specify the links between task hierarchy, task-oriented specification, software architecture and code documents aiming at improving co-evolutionary design. Vanderdonckt [21] defines a mapping model that contains the mappings between UI models and their elements. It is not in the scope of this paper to detail or compare different mapping techniques, since most of them aim for UI generation and focus on UI design artifacts, different from our intended goals. But we consider them as a support for model mapping and traceability between the models.

2.3   BP Models and UI Models

BP models are associated with UI models through task models, seen in Figure 1 (it depicts the mappings between the models, not the content). Each level of the BP is mapped with the different levels in the task model, which is associated with UI components: *screen group*, a group of closely related screens and possible sub-groups to precisely classify screens; *screen*, a state of the user interaction where it is possible to perform a task or part of a task or even several tasks; *screen fragment*, a container of related elements in the screen; *screen element*, the most atomic component to perform user tasks (e.g. input or display data, navigate). UI components are linked to the final UI. The methodology is flexible enough to enable stakeholders (e.g. business analysts, UI designers) to specify at which level of granularity they will map the elements, depending on the complexity of the processes and systems, on the information available and other aspects that directly influence the impact analysis.

We have specified how these models are linked to support impact analysis when changes are requested in any of these models. The changes may happen in different directions: forward and backward approaches, in which the actions of stakeholders to change the models are organized in phases related to business process improvement methodologies (Process improvement) and User-Centered Design (User and Task Analysis, Conceptual Design, UI Design, Usability Test), as seen in Figure 1.

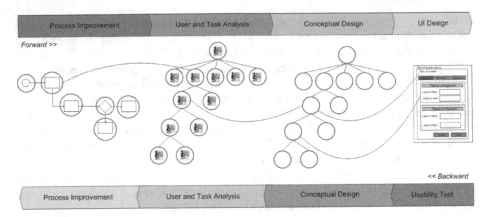

Fig. 1. Approaches used in the association of business processes with user interfaces

In the forward approach, changes on BPs may impact task models and UIs. It helps identifying what impact the optimization of processes has on the user interaction. Such changes can be done from a variety of reasons: new or alternative ways of doing things, new business opportunities, organizational changes, new regulations; etc. In the backward approach, changes on UIs may impact task models and BPs. It helps identifying how the improved usability of UIs suggested by systems users (e.g. customers, employees) impacts BPs. Reasons for such changes include defects to be fixed, better user understanding of the systems' features, new technology, etc.

We defined a set of rules to support the impact analysis by associating every BP model element with a UI element via a task model; this fine-grained granularity expresses details in the results of the impact analysis. With these rules, we can analyze: when a node is changed, what can be done in the other models to maintain alignment (e.g. when a screen is deleted, the related activity is no longer supported). The traceability is demonstrated by navigating in the chain of links, so when a node in a model is selected, the traceability lists what is related to it in the other models.

3   Managing Models

This framework is adaptable to changes in the organizational context, thus it accepts that the way processes are modeled and structured in different layers may change and that the philosophy of user interaction may be evolved, thus leading to the need to update how these core models are managed. For this purpose, we have selected an expert system approach based on production rules, where these rules specify how these models are managed to provide more flexibility. Rules support a rich representation of first-order logic to describe general knowledge about a certain domain [16]. The domain has a knowledge representation, whose elements are linked through formal symbols to compose rules as a collection of propositions [5]. There are many rule engines available on the market and open source as well. Most of them can be embedded in applications, allowing them to execute their own rules and get benefit from the decision-making features. In our case, when there are changes in the structure of the models that impact the form of managing them, the rules can be directly updated, without the need for maintenance of the traceability tool.

The basic properties of transformation rules are [12]: *tunability*, the possibility to adapt the transformation by parameters; *traceability*, the possibility to trace one element in the target model back to its causing element in the source model; *incremental consistency*, information added manually to the target model is not overwritten if the transformation is executed again (e.g. after the model is updated); *bidirectionality*, transformation applied from source to target and vice-versa.

As a contribution, we have defined 3 types of rules that adhere to these properties:

1. *Transformation*: transform BPMN [13] business processes in task models;
2. *Change Management*: do impact analysis of changes made on the models;
3. *Verification*: maintain consistency in the links of tasks with UI components.

These rules have been defined based on the links between the models, as explained in the previous section. The specific mapping between BP elements and task model elements have been presented and detailed in [18]. The mapping between BP and task model elements has been assessed through the association of: BPMN core elements (flow objects, connecting objects, artifacts) with task relationships (e.g. sequence flow with enabling and enabling with information passing); BP activity attributes with task properties (e.g. conditional flow with optional task); and process task type with task type (e.g. service task with application task). Such an assessment enabled the identification of similarities in the semantics of these two notations and the different aspects that may indicate a prospective need of adaptation in one them. For example, a Data-Based Exclusive Gateway represents that only one of the various paths can be taken and it can be represented as a deterministic choice between tasks in the task model, but for this representation to be complete, it is necessary to allocate a condition for each target task in the task model, not only a condition in the relationship between two tasks because each target activity in a gateway can have a different condition. In addition, such associations depict a many-to-many mapping between BPMN and task model elements as depicted in the association of both BPMN 'sub-processes' and 'tasks' to 'tasks' in the task model; and the association of BPMN 'sequence flow' to both 'enabling' and 'enabling with information passing' in the task model, depending on the condition type of the sequence flow; etc.

From these mappings, we have defined 53 transformation and change management rules; each of them has been explored for four different operations, totalizing in 212 rules for forward engineering. For this paper, we focus on the transformation and change management rules that have been written using the Drools [11] rule language.

To demonstrate how the alignment is achieved, the rules are explained using the context of customers requesting insurance contracts, from a case study with a large bank-insurance organization [18]. In this context, when aiming to increase customer satisfaction and optimize the performance of enterprise operations (with a more efficient service through faster responses), business analysts decided to allow customers to follow the status of their requests. This improvement has impacts spread in users' tasks and UIs of different systems in the forward and backward approaches, illustrated in the following sub-sections.

3.1 Forward Approach

In the forward approach, we demonstrate how changes on BPs have impacts on task models and UI components. Note that the IDs used in the rules are abstract illustrations of the elements (e.g. "sF-LogIn-ViewRequest") to help in their understanding, they are not real representations of the IDs saved on the knowledge base (e.g. UUID = d79d24ec0c6d4ba5b08f9cf911512f78).

From Business to Task. For each element updated in a BP model, there is a rule that transforms it into an element in the task model. These rules are classified in operations that represent actions performed on BP elements that result on actions that must be executed on task models (Table 1). The intent is to consider different types of operations that can change BPs and execute the existing rules at design time to maintain the alignment, exemplified in this paper with one rule for each operation. The first rule is presented both in natural language and in the Drools rule language for demonstration; the other examples are presented only in natural language for clarity.

Table 1. Classification of operations

Operation	Definition	Action on BPMN element	Change on task model	Impact on UI components
Add	To include an element	Create element	Create TM element	Create UI component
Delete	To remove an element	Remove element	Remove TM element	Remove UI component
Modify	To change the attributes of an element	Change type of element Change name of element	Update TM element Change name of TM element	Update UI component Change name of UI component
Order	To arrange elements	Change sequence of activities	Change sequence of tasks	Change sequence of UI component
Merge	To unite elements	Remove element	Remove TM element	Remove UI component
		Change type of element	Update TM element	Update UI component
		Change name of element	Change name of TM element	Change name of UI component
Split	To divide or separate elements	Change type of element	Update TM element	Update UI component
		Change name of element	Change name of TM element	Change name of UI component
		Create element	Create TM element	Create UI component
Decompose	To separate into constituent elements	Create element	Create TM element	Create UI component

In the BPs for insurance contracts, in order to enable customers to follow the status of requests, business analysts have created a new sub-process called 'Follow request status'. This sub-process is composed of tasks informing that customers can login into the *insurance contract online system* and then view the request status. For each of the newly created tasks and their associations in the sub-process, rules for the operation 'Add' are executed to create the equivalent elements in the task model. For the operation **'Add'**, the following rule is executed, which expressed in natural language means that: "When a default sequence flow (with a specific id) linking two tasks (e.g. source task 'Log in' and target task 'View request') is created in a BP, then it results in creating an enabling relationship linking the two equivalent tasks in the task model":

```
rule "AddBPMNSequenceFlow"
when
    s: SequenceFlow(id == "sF-LogIn-ViewRequest")
then
    insert(new Enabling(s.getId(),s.getSourceRef(),s.getTargetRef()));
end
```

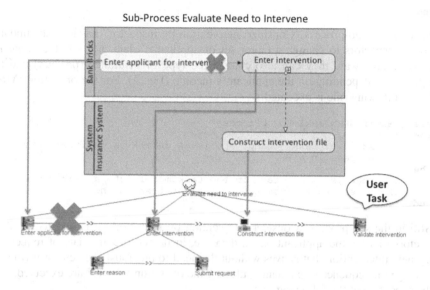

Fig. 2. Task deleted from the sub-process and its equivalent deleted task in the task model

Besides that, business analysts have also decided to improve the internal communication so the customer can acknowledge the status updates more efficiently. They have decided that the bank agents do not need to enter interventions through a different form; it is enough to enter the reasoning within the insurance contract request. The sub-processes "Evaluate need to intervene" and "Consider intervention by inspector" are directly impacted by this strategic decision.

First, the sub-process "Evaluate need to intervene" needs to have the task "Enter applicant intervention" removed since there is no longer a specific form for intervention requests (Fig. 2). To delete this task and its relationships in the task model, rules for the operation 'Delete' are executed. Note that this figure shows the task model evolved with a user task, not relevant for the business process, but important for user interaction. When the BP is changed and the task model is regenerated by executing the rules, this extra user task must remain to guarantee incremental consistency; reason for adopting an incremental transformation approach [12], which updates the changed elements with the newly generated ones, keeping the extra elements and the unchanged elements untouched.

For the operation **'Delete'**, the following rule is executed to delete a task and its relationship:

```
rule "DeleteBPMNTask"
when
       a task (i.e. 'Enter applicant for intervention') and its se-
       quence flow are removed from BP
then
       remove the equivalent task (with the same id of task) and ena-
       bling relationship (with the same id of sequence flow) from the
       task model
end
```

Second, the sub-process "Consider intervention by inspector" has its tasks updated to allow inspectors to change a larger set of applicants' data, not just the value for insurance. This way, they can also change the type of insurance (product) and the charged taxes depending on the applicant's income (Fig. 3). For the operation **'Modify'**, the following rule is executed:

```
rule "ModifyBPMNTaskIntoSubProcess"
when
       a task (i.e. task 'Change applicant data') is modified into a
       sub-process in a BP
then
       change this atomic task in the task model into a task composed
       of the sub-tasks from the equivalent task in the BP
end
```

Still in the sub-process "Consider intervention by inspector", it is updated to allow inspectors to view the applicant name, data file, insurance file and date of request for every new intervention that arrives without the need to previously search for it (Fig. 3). To change the sequence of elements, rules for the operation **'Order'** are executed, such as the execution of the following rule:

```
rule "OrderBPMNSequenceFlow"
when
     the order of two tasks (i.e. 'Search for applicant' and 'View
     applicant data') is changed in a BP
then
     change the order of the equivalent tasks in the task model
end
```

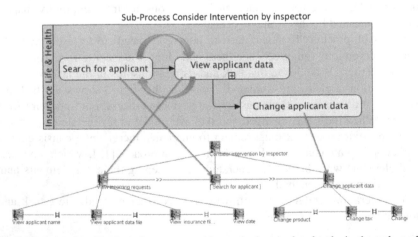

Fig. 3. Tasks updated in the sub-process and its equivalent updated tasks in the task model

Concerning the other operations, we consider that operations to merge, split and decompose elements are resulting from a collection of the previously mentioned operations. For instance, to **merge** two sub-processes in a BP, one of the sub-processes is deleted (e.g. call Rule *DeleteBPMNSubProcess*) and the other one is modified, such as changing its name (e.g. call Rule *ModifyBPMNSubProcessName*). An example to **split** one sub-process in two sub-processes, the existing sub-process is modified (e.g. call Rule *ModifyBPMNSubProcessName*), a new one is created (e.g. call Rule *AddBPMNSubProcess*) and a link between them is created (e.g. call Rule *AddBPMNSequenceFlow*). To **decompose** one sub-process in tasks, for each new task created within the sub-process, a new sub-task is created within the equivalent task in the task model (e.g. call Rule *ModifyBPMNSubProcessWithSubTasks*). When any of these operations are performed on BP elements, the consequent actions are performed on the task model elements and UI components that have been linked to the updated BP elements. After the rules are executed and task models are aligned with the updated business processes, a new set of rules are executed in order to maintain alignment with UIs, explained as follows.

From Task to UI. Since the task model is mapped to UI components; for each element changed in a task model, there is a rule that indicates which UI components should be updated accordingly. These rules are classified in operations (Table 1) that represent actions performed on task model elements that result on advices, which could be manually done on UIs by UI designers/usability experts.

To exemplify that, still in the intervention of insurance contracts (as a continuation of the rules related to Fig. 3), inspectors view all incoming requests then decide to either search for a specific applicant or directly change the data of an applicant among the incoming requests. In this scenario, the order of tasks has been changed and the type of one task has been updated to a sub-process (Fig. 4). First, for the operation 'Order', the following rule is executed:

```
rule "OrderTMEnabling"
when
    the order of two tasks (i.e. 'Viewing incoming requests' and
    'Search for applicant') is changed in the task model
then
    change the order of the UI components that are linked to these
    tasks (i.e. two screen fragments 'View incoming requests' and
    'Search for applicant')
end
```

Second, for the operation **'Modify'**, the following rule is executed:

```
rule "ModifyTMAtomicUITaskIntoSubTasks"
when
    an atomic task (i.e. 'Change of applicant data') is modified
    into a task composed of sub-tasks in the task model
then
    add screen elements for each of the added sub-tasks (e.g.
    'Change product', 'Change tax') in the screen fragment that is
    linked to this updated task (i.e. screen fragment 'Financial
    data' of the screen 'Change data')
end
```

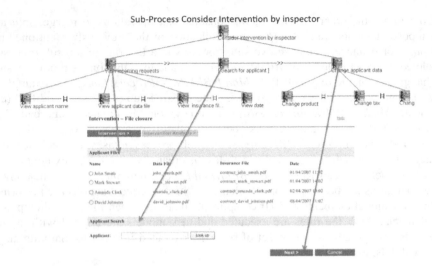

Fig. 4. Tasks updated in the task model and its equivalent updated UI

Another example for the operation 'Modify' is when two sub-tasks are first linked with 'Concurrency' relationship, then this operator is changed to an 'Enabling' relationship in the task model; the consequent change in the UI is that the updated UI should reflect the sequence by organizing the related UI components in two screens or in two screen fragments that are navigable as a wizard.

To summarize with a general overview of changes, the process 'Closure' was updated to provide transparent information for customers and more productivity with internal communication. This change has resulted in updating four sub-processes for a core product in the bank (Fig. 5). Changes on these sub-processes were processed in the task models that were adequately evolved to consider the user interaction. The updated task models were then processed in order to indicate exactly which UIs components (linked to users' tasks) were impacted from such changes. Before changes are made, the traceability enables impact analysis by allowing stakeholders to navigate in the chain of links and visualize which UIs could be impacted if any change is made on specific BPs as suggested by business analysts.

The impact analysis resulted in suggesting the following changes: 1) The screen 'File Closure' has now a new screen fragment 'intervention' composed of two screen elements to allow bank agents to inform the reason and to do the request in the same screen, therefore; 2) There is no need for the screen 'Enter Intervention' with a specific form that added burocracy; 3) In the screen 'Consider Intervention', its screen fragments were updated by changing their order; 4) The screen 'Change data' has more screen elements in screen fragment 'applicant data' that gave more flexibility to inspectors; and 5) The screen 'Follow Request' was created in the insurance contract online system to allow customers to follow the status of their requests. Now, we examine when changes start on UIs through the backward approach.

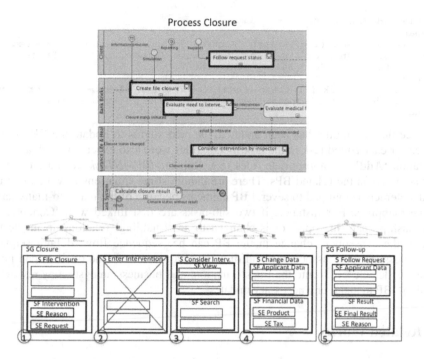

Fig. 5. Overview of the impact analysis considering BPs, task models and UI components

3.2 Backward Approach

The UI-Business alignment framework also adheres to the property of *bidirectionality*, which means that the transformation can be applied not only from source to target but also backwards from target to source [12]. The backward approach is applied when users of enterprise systems suggest improvements on UIs or point out issues that interfere with the progress of their work. This opens a new channel for business process improvement that can start with actual users (bank employees using the system at the bank agency or customers using electronic system on the web at home) who aid to increase productivity within the organization.

To exemplify the context of the backward approach, we present a set of change scenarios: after some weeks using the updated systems, some requests arrived from users at the bank agencies. For the screen 'File Closure', agents requested the screen fragment 'Intervention' to be retracted by default so they can expand it just when necessary. For the screen 'Consider Intervention', inspectors requested to add the screen fragment 'search' also on the top of the screen because there are usually too many incoming requests on this screen. For the insurance contract online system, customers asked to be able to request a second review and send extra documentation (e.g. work contract, bank statement, salary statement) to prove specific financial data in order to improve the type of insurance they want to receive.

To address this request, a new screen was created, named 'Request Second Opinion' and the task model was updated. With the operation **'Add'**, the following rule is executed:

```
rule "AddUIScreen"
when
    a new screen (i.e. Screen 'Request Second Opinion') is created
    with screen elements (i.e. 'Send-Work-Contract', 'Send-Bank-
    Statement', 'Send-Salary-Statement')
then
    create a task for the new screen and a set of sub-tasks for each
    of the created screen elements within the related screen
end
```

Once the task model has been updated, the next step is to update the BPs accordingly. For each added task in the task model, rules were also executed; such as for the operation **'Add'**, the appropriate rules (e.g. Rule *AddBPMNTask*) added the equivalent activities in the related BPs. There are though some situations in which one task model element is mapped to several BP elements because of the many-to-many nature of the mappings. For instance, if two sub-tasks are first linked with 'Concurrency' relationship, then this operator is changed to an 'Enabling' relationship in the task model; the consequent change in the BP can be: sequence flow, default sequence flow, message flow, association and directional association. One of them can be selected as default to execute the transformation, and business analysts may review the resulting BP to make any necessary updates.

4 Related Works

Recent works propose different types of technological support for traceability between business processes and the supporting software systems, such as [2]. Among them, the Center of Organizational Engineering (CEO) Framework represents an enterprise architecture that aligns the organization's strategy with its business processes, people and IT software and hardware [17], with a differential on adding people to this strategy.

Artifact-Centered Operational Modeling (ACOM) is an approach to capture business operational knowledge that is distinguished from other approaches by identifying one information structure, the artifact that travels from end to end in a process. It can be understood as an alternative to more familiar approaches, such as process modeling, differentiated by managing progress toward goals [4].

The Model Information Flow used at SAP [3] follows a model-driven approach that uses models and transformations between them for defining, deploying and managing SAP applications. It is noted that the models in the chain, after the business process model is customized for a project, are mostly related to IT infrastructure, for instance models to describe internal structure of the software, demand for resources by components, resource infrastructure configurations, etc.

One of the researches on the enhancement of the UI design practice with business process modeling [19] points out the importance of model-based UI design automation in scenarios with intensive business process that give rise to systems with lots of data entering and display, and role-specific UIs.

The researched strategies that align business processes and systems focus on information system architecture, considering information system and technological services, IT infrastructure, application platform and technological/software components. Even though there are recent works on the alignment of business processes with user-centered design and development, they tend to focus on specific technologies, such as web-based applications [15], even though they advocate for a hybrid approach combining task models and process models; while others define structures for associating business processes and UIs with direct links, such as [20]. On the other hand, we envision a more flexible approach with the use of conceptual models to facilitate interoperability of solutions; and considering users' tasks that are primordial for designing UIs that are easy to use and contribute to increase the productivity of professionals in organizations when doing their daily work constantly interacting with enterprise systems.

5 Conclusion

This paper presented a model-driven approach to link BP and UI models. With this approach, models are mapped in order to more efficiently propagate changes when needed. In addition, the user perspective is considered in alignment with business needs. In more details, we demonstrated how our proposal is suitable for the context of a large bank/insurance organization. This research has proposed a framework for UI-Business Alignment that is practical, user-centered, and adaptable to specific organizational structures, human-centered and provides model traceability.

As future work, in order to assess the application of this framework in a different business domain, we are applying this framework in a telecommunications large company in which we will be able to evaluate the integration of the UI-Business Alignment strategy with their software development process, the execution of the rules in a project related to one of the products with good visibility in the organization, and the acceptance of the stakeholders involved with the solution.

Acknowledgments. We gratefully acknowledge the support of the Program Alban, the European Union Program of High Level Scholarships for Latin America, under scholarship number E06D103843BR.

References

1. Aberdeen Group. Aligning IT to Business Process: How BPM is Complementing ERP and Custom Applications. Research Brief. Abardeen Group (2007)
2. Ali, M.F., Pérez-Quiñones, M.A., Abrams, M.: Building Multi-Platform User Interfaces with UIML. In: Multiple User Interfaces: Engineering and Application Framework. John Wiley and Sons, New York (2003)
3. Belrose, G., Brand, K., Edwards, N., Graupner, S.: Business-driven IT for SAP – The Model Information Flow. In: Proceedings of the Second IEEE/IFIP International Workshop on Business-Driven IT Management (2007)
4. Bhattacharya, K., Caswell, N., Kumaran, S., Nigam, A., Wu, F.: Artifact-centric Operational Modeling: Lessons learned from customer engagements. IBM Systems Journal 46, 4 (2007)
5. Brachman, R.J., Levesque, H.J.: Knowledge Representation and Reasoning. Elsevier, Amsterdam (2004)
6. Brown, J., Graham, T.C.N., Wright, T.: The Vista Environment for the Coevolutionary Design of User Interfaces. In: CHI 1998, pp. 376–383 (1998)

7. Calvary, G., Coutaz, J., Thevenin, D., Limbourg, Q., Bouillon, L., Vanderdonckt, J.: A Unifying Reference Framework for Multi-Target User Interfaces. Interacting with Computers 15(3), 289–308 (2003)
8. Davenport, T.: Process Innovation: Reengineering work through information technology. Harvard Business School Press, Boston (1993)
9. Henderson, J.C., Venkatraman, N.: Strategic Alignment: Leveraging information technology for transforming organizations. IBM Systems Journal 38(2&3) (1999)
10. Henry, P.: Process-User Interface Alignment: New Value From a New Level of Alignment. Align Journal (2007)
11. JBoss Drools, http://www.jboss.org/drools
12. Kleppe, A., Warmer, J., Bast, W.: MDA Explained: The Model Driven Architecture: Practice and Promise. Addison-Wesley Professional, Reading (2003)
13. OMG Business Process Modeling Notation Specification v1.1, http://www.omg.org/spec/BPMN/1.1/PDF
14. Paternò, F., Santoro, C.: A unified method for designing interactive systems adaptable to mobile and stationary platforms. Interacting with Computers 15(3), 349–366 (2003)
15. Pontico, F., Farenc, C., Winckler, M.: Model-Based support for specifying eService eGovernment Applications. In: Coninx, K., Luyten, K., Schneider, K.A. (eds.) TAMODIA 2006. LNCS, vol. 4385, pp. 54–67. Springer, Heidelberg (2007)
16. Russel, S., Norvig, P.: Artificial Intelligence – A Modern Approach. Prentice-Hall, Englewood Cliffs (2003)
17. Sousa, P., Caetano, A., Vasconcelos, A., Pereira, C., Tribolet, J.: Enterprise Architecture Modelling with the Unified Modelling Language 2.0. In: Ritten, P. (ed.) Enterprise Modelling and Computing with UML. IRM Press, Hershey (2006)
18. Sousa, K., Mendonça, H., Vanderdonckt, J.: A Model-Driven Approach to Align Business Processes with User Interfaces. International Journal of Universal Computer Science, Special issue on Human-Computer Interaction14(19), 3236–3249 (2008); Gallud, J.A., Lozano, M. (eds.)
19. Sukaviriya, N., Sinha, V., Ramachandra, T., Mani, S., Stolze, M.: User-centered Design and Business Process Modeling: Cross Road in Rapid Prototyping Tools. In: Baranauskas, C., Palanque, P., Abascal, J., Barbosa, S.D.J. (eds.) INTERACT 2007. LNCS, vol. 4662, pp. 165–178. Springer, Heidelberg (2007)
20. Traetteberg, H.: UI Design without a Task Modeling Language – Using BPMN and Diamodl for Task Modeling and Dialog Design. In: Forbrig, P., Paternò, F. (eds.) HCSE/TAMODIA 2008. LNCS, vol. 5247, pp. 110–117. Springer, Heidelberg (2008)
21. Vanderdonckt, J.: A MDA-Compliant Environment for Developing User Interfaces of Information Systems. In: Pastor, Ó., Falcão e Cunha, J. (eds.) CAiSE 2005. LNCS, vol. 3520, pp. 16–31. Springer, Heidelberg (2005)

Towards Intuitive Modeling of Business Processes: Prospects for Flow- and Natural-Language Orientation

Matthias Neubauer, Stefan Oppl, and Christian Stary

Johannes Kepler University Linz,
Department of Business Information Systems – Communications Engineering,
Freistädter Straße 315, 4040 Linz, Austria
{Matthias.Neubauer,Stefan.Oppl,Christian.Stary}@jku.at

Abstract. As organizations need to adapt constantly, it becomes increasingly important for stakeholders to start talking a 'business-process language' – they need to develop an understanding of processes in terms of intertwining work structure and behavior information. The closer business-process modeling techniques are to mental representations of their users, i.e. the more intuitively models can be created and communicated, the more effectively models can be utilized in the course of change processes. In our empirical study we were interested in adequately supporting participatory management of change based on business process models. The stakeholders' individual cognitive work load should be minimal when explicating and sharing process knowledge. In the study individuals not familiar with modeling were introduced to the idea of business-process modeling, and asked to model a given scenario. We also asked them to use a notation with open semantics to enable authentic representations. The results show in the majority of cases flow-oriented understanding of business-process modeling, and in some cases natural language orientation. The data suggest providing respective modeling techniques and tools for organizational development.

Keywords: Human factors in modeling, business-process modeling, intuitive representation.

1 Introduction

A rapidly changing whilst competitive business environment forces organizations to respond through enterprise transformations on the structural level ([2], [17]). Information systems and the prevalent processes need to reflect the changes. Performing these representational and technological adaptations is not trivial, as '*human cognition often perceives dynamic phenomena by developing a series of snapshots, capturing the true dynamics inherent on a process is challenging. By mistakenly taking snapshots to represent processes, there is a risk of tinkering with the wrong things, destroying natural controls that already exists, and essentially turning the organization into a jumbled mess of confusion*' [20] (cited in [12], p.15). One way to avoid this endangering situation for organizations is to provide representation schemes for business processes as a means for documentation and mutual information exchange. Such an endeavor is even

D. England et al. (Eds.): TAMODIA 2009, LNCS 5963, pp. 15–27, 2010.
© Springer-Verlag Berlin Heidelberg 2010

more important in inherently networked organizational settings where stakeholders collaborate in different locations in an asynchronous way ([1], p.37).

Various ways for expressing and representing process-related information are used depending on the expertise and work domain of the persons involved in organizational work and change processes:

- Natural language, as mainly being used by operational staff members
- Business-process modeling languages, as being used by organizational developers and by domain experts
- Formal specification languages and programming languages, as being used by information-system developers and technology experts.

Enabling mutual understanding is not only prevented by the use of syntactically different representation forms, but also by different semantics applied to representational schemes even of the same kind [15]. As business-process models, and thus business-process modeling languages, should bridge the gap between domain knowledge, organizational structures, and technology (cf. [16]), they should not only be individually intelligible for all stakeholders, but rather empower them to share meaning and negotiate models on a common level of understanding. Most of the existing languages approach this requirement by a detailed specification of both, structure and meaning of their notational elements ([11], pp. 49-58). However, *a multitude of concepts surround the proper definition of complex modeling languages, and many people are confused about what these concepts – both crucial and marginal – really mean and how to understand and use them. This confusion is particularly apparent in the context of UML, [...] but is also characteristic of other modeling approaches'* [6].

Striving to overcome the resulting lack of meaningful modeling a certain type of organization, the 'sense-and-respond organization' has been envisioned [8]. Moreover, some effort to categorize modeling misconceptions has been spent (cf. [2], [3], and [18]), however, without significant impact on the design of modeling languages. Most of currently available modeling languages are neither user- nor domain-oriented. In addition, they still lack the ability to adapt semantics of language elements to local contexts or multiple (user-) perspectives ([11], p.61).

Hence, our study intended to identify factors that cause confusion, and thus, cognitive work load in the course of modeling, preventing the alignment of individual perspectives. We investigated notational constructs that allow generating adequate business-process models from a stakeholder perspective, by studying how those constructs are utilized in the course of modeling.

Addressing cognitive factors of business-process modeling in this way, several other factors of organizational development and change are affected (cf. [14]):

- Economic factors, such as costs and transformation effort – the efficiency of modeling processes could be increased through stakeholder-oriented techniques.
- Social factors, such as conflicts, and negotiations about the meaning of representations – interactions can become more focused using intuitive model elements and languages to describe business processes.

- Organizational factors, such as iterations, social tensions, and mutual quality control – they can be minimized when not burdening stakeholders with confusing notations and model conceptions.

In section 2 we detail the design of the study, and its implementation. In section 3 we discuss the results, and relate them to reported empirical work from the field. Section 4 concludes the paper, summarizing our objectives and results, and sketching our future research.

2 The Study

In section 2.1 the elements needed to be taking into account for the design of the investigation are introduced, before the setting is explained in detail. In section 2.2 we report on actually performing the field study.

2.1 Design

When organizational changes or information systems based on business processes are projected, a variety of data and perspectives have to be collected, integrated, documented, and reflected. They typically comprise (cf. [5], [7]):

- features of support instruments and tools
- information structures
- conditions of use and semantic relationships concerning personal and organizational resources
- events triggering modifications and change resources that are available or anticipated
- competences and skills required for task accomplishment

These categories represent perceived demands based on individual experiences as well as envisioned ones, as change processes tackle the current situation and envisioned ones. The stakeholders, involved in explication and reflection, likely represent different perspectives according to their functional role, among them:

- responsible, e.g. project manager
- organizational developer, such as process owner and case manager
- information system or software developer
- (knowledge) worker

Modeling sessions address both, the above mentioned categories of organizational data, and the various perspectives of stakeholders. Adequate models are expected to represent and support the individual and collective access to organizational knowledge as perceived by stakeholders. Hence, models, either in diagrammatic or other form, are used for

- explicating, expressing, documenting, forming, memorizing, and rearranging
- ideas, settled thought, general knowledge, dedicated information as well as open issues.

They serve as individual container as well as collective resource which can be used by all stakeholders to handle both, already consolidated information, and codified knowledge that still needs to be consolidated. As the study has been intended to find out constructs and procedures adequate[1] for humans, in order to facilitate meaningful modeling, we needed to use an open language format. Moreover, dynamic switching between particular elements or views on models, such as processes, functions, tasks, should help avoiding any bias when stakeholders were modeling. Nevertheless, the integration/combination of different elements and views within a single representation is of major importance, as processes depict different aspects (including mutual relationships) of an organization. Finally, the representation of incomplete or uncertain information should enable modelers to focus on individually reliable knowledge rather than speculative descriptions. However, indicating incompleteness might trigger other individuals to share their view with the original model creator(s).

As the development of SeeMe [10] has been driven by the human factors mentioned above, we have decided to use this language in this study. It allows to document individual points of view on a topic in collective settings. Due to its constructs (see section 2.2) it can be used in the early phases of socio-technical solution development in a transparent way. It fits settings where interactions between individual stakeholders are going to be supported and shaped by ICT albeit its semi-structuredness. The latter is relevant when eliciting and codifying knowledge about business processes (in collaborative settings).

SeeMe has been developed after it had turned out that existing diagrammatic modeling methods did not support the design of socio-technical systems in a constructive way. In contrast to other approaches to diagrammatic modeling, such as EPCs [16], SeeMe provides constructs to express vagueness and allows individual semantic representations in a given context (cf. [9], [10]). It is used in scenarios where relevant stakeholders get together to elicit and exchange their knowledge on some socio-technical issue.

In the study we asked students in business computing to contribute to a common scenario, namely purchasing a car – a procedure that occurs when developing automotive web shops in a user-centred way. We expected a variety of aspects that should become visible when documenting the relevant process. According to the theoretical background of SeeMe, namely communication theory, we expected stakeholders not only to communicate apparent details regarding purchasing a car, but also essential but hidden or primarily intangible assets. The latter are required for adequate representations, as they provide valuable input for organizational development and corresponding technological artefacts.

This setting should lead to modeling styles and patterns which represent the variety of business-process aspects while still allowing stakeholders to focus on the essential aspects of the task scenario. We did not force stakeholders to detail all process knowledge with respect to tools and information elements when modeling. They were able and encouraged to model incomplete or uncertain information, which could have been detailed later on.

---

[1] "Adequate for humans" means to allow individuals expressing and representing their knowledge with cognitive effort not burdening them when using a modeling language to the extent they consider relevant.

In line with SeeMe applications so far, the resulting process diagrams were expected to capture

- actors, tasks, support tools, and content required for task accomplishment
- their relationships as perceived by the stakeholders
- different perspective expressed through different (types) of relationships
- different arrangements of process elements
- different levels of detail or granularity
- current and envisioned scenarios
- formal and informal structures
- technical, cognitive, and social aspects
- incomplete and vague specification
- patterns and conventions.

Hence, the exploratory study should lead to the identification of constructs, within a certain scenario of use, and methodological inputs on how to use individually selected constructs in the course of modeling. Both inputs could challenge the effectiveness of existing business-process modeling languages and tools, and thus, the efficiency of modeling sessions using existing languages and tools. By identifying only elements and modeling steps considered to be essential for a shared understanding when accomplishing work tasks or envisioning organizational changes, novel types of languages and/or forms of interaction could emerge.

2.2 Implementation

We have performed 52 individual modeling sessions with different business computing students from the Johannes Kepler University Linz. The study has been conducted in an undergraduate lab on business-process modeling. The participating students had no prior formal education in business-process modeling and have been provided with input on SeeMe constructs and some procedural instructions to complete the study task. Besides theory input, a textual example of a car-buying process has been prepared.

The following SeeMe constructs have been introduced to the participants of the study (cf. [10]):

- Role
- Activity
- Entity
- Embedding of elements
- Vagueness/Incompleteness
- Default meaning of relations among elements
- Connectors (AND, OR, XOR, Unspecified)
- Modifiers

In addition, the subsequent procedural instructions have been given to the participants:

1. Collect relevant basic elements (role, activity, entity) based on the text description of the case.

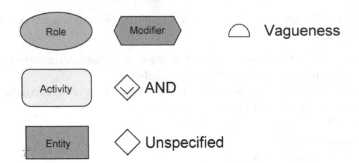

Fig. 1. Subset of SeeMe modeling constructs used in the modeling examples of section 3

2. Identify relations between the selected basic elements, starting with relations between basic elements of one type, and continuing with relations between basic elements of different types.
3. Identify situations where connectors are needed according to your under-standing.
4. Try to capture as many aspects of the textual process description as possible in the diagrammatic SeeMe model.

In order to analyze the models, the following data have been recorded:

- Modeling styles and patterns
- Usage of modeling constructs

Modeling styles and patterns describe flavors of models and constructs directing the modeling process, such as flow orientation. Flow orientation considers modeling of the activity-flow within the given process. It also includes the usage of connectors, for instance to model optional or parallel activity-flows.

Besides flow orientation, we have investigated the orientation towards natural-language structures, since humans traditionally use natural language to describe their view upon business processes. With respect to natural language orientation we evalu-ated, whether modelers have utilized SeeMe constructs to express sentence semantics, such as subject-predicate-object. In this context the subject represents the starting point of an action, the predicate the action to be taken, and the object the target of the action.

In addition, we had a look at the usage of modeling constructs themselves. We have checked the frequency of each modeling construct in the created models to dis-cover patterns of use. Finally, we have captured the meaning modelers have assigned to modeling constructs in the course of knowledge elicitation and sharing.

The data have been collected and evaluated in spring term (March 09 to June 09). All students have accomplished the task within one week and delivered SeeMe mod-els for the process of purchasing a car.

As we investigated the modeling results and patterns of using modeling elements focusing on complete models, we neither collected additional background information nor specific information about the modeling process itself. Hence, we did not record variables such as knowing other notations. Effects due to the selection of the scenario have also not been measured.

3 Results and Discussion

After presenting the results in a structured way in section 3.1, we interpret them in the context of other studies on cognitive factors and our objectives in section 3.2.

3.1 Results

The data has been analyzed from a construct and usage perspective. The first perspective focuses on the categories of constructs that have been used in the course of modeling. The latter allows insights in the process of modeling, in particular clustering with respect to modeling styles and patterns.

Semantic Constructs
In the study all of the stakeholders have used the following constructs according to the SeeMe notation:

- Role
- Activity
- Entity
- Standard relations between elements
- Vagueness/Incompleteness

Furthermore, the majority (96%) of the participants has used the embodiment concept of SeeMe, i.e. sub-elements, that are part of a super-element. Since SeeMe allows embedding elements of different types into one another (cf. [10]), we also have looked for element types that are primarily used as container for others. Considering the semantics of embedding different element-types, [10] recommends to embed an element when it is mainly relevant for a single element different from the considered one (which indicates encapsulation).

Our results show that embedding of sub-activities in activities has dominated the modeling process. In 92 percent of the models this kind of modeling construct has been applied, whereas in only 50 percent of the models embedding of entities in activities could be found. Similarly, half of the modelers have utilized embedding of entities in other entities. In about 25 percent of the models sub-roles have been embedded in roles, whereas 20 percent of the modelers have embedded roles in activities. 12 percent of the participants have modeled sub-entities within roles, and 10 percent sub-activities within entities. Only about 4 percent have arranged sub-activities within roles and sub-roles within entities.

In addition to the embodiment concept, the majority of the modelers (85%) have utilized connectors. Connectors allow expressing interdependencies between standard relations, e.g. activity A is followed by activity B OR C. SeeMe does not restrict the usage of connectors to a specific relation type, and therefore we have also scanned the models with respect to the context and type of connectors. We have found out that connectors have primarily been used to control the flow of activities (in 56% of the models), e.g. to represent optional activities or parallel activities within a process. Half of the modelers have used connectors to represent interdependencies between relations of entities, e.g. an activity requires document B AND document A. Further usage of connectors has been analyzed considering roles. 19 percent of the participants have used connectors in combination with relations of roles, e.g. Joe Public OR Jane Public is purchasing a car.

The usage of modifiers has also been target of our investigation. In SeeMe, modifiers are intended to annotate basic elements, such as activities, roles and entities, and relations to express conditions and events. In our study 60 percent of the modelers have used modifiers for annotation.

Procedural Issues

As described above, the participants were given only basic procedural instructions. Considering the modeling results, the following model characteristics could be observed:

- The majority (90%) of participants has modeled the process flow from top to bottom, i.e. activities have been arranged from top to bottom. Roles and entities associated with specific activities were placed next to the activities
- 10 percent of the modelers have decided to arrange the process flow from left to right. They have positioned activities in the middle of the diagram, roles above activities and entities below activities. Herrmann [10] proposes such a layout for models built with SeeMe.
- The modeling results differ significantly in the level of detail, ranging from vague and high-level descriptions to concrete process steps.
- The majority (85%) of the modelers has depicted the concrete process description and has not generated an abstract picture of the process.

Modeling Styles and Patterns

We have identified the following three model categories when analyzing the style of modeling:

- Flow-oriented models
- Natural language-oriented models
- Mixed models

Flow-oriented Modeling Examples

Most of the specified processes show a flow orientation. Overall, 69 percent of the modeling results are flow-orientated. With regard to the utilized SeeMe constructs we have made several observations when analyzing the flow-oriented models.

The embodiment concept of SeeMe has been utilized frequently. Primarily, subactivities have been embedded in activities (by a rate of 97%), followed by subentities. The latter have been assigned either to super-activities or super-entities (44%), and sub-roles which were related to super-roles (19%). Further forms of embodiment have been the assignment of sub-roles to activities (11%), and sub-entities to roles (8%). Embedding of activities in roles or entities as well as roles in entities have hardly been used (3%).

Connectors could be found in the majority (83%) of the flow-oriented models, whereas they were mainly set between activities to control the process flow (61%). In contrast to these results, 42 percent of the process models contain connectors between entities, and only 8 percent contain connectors between roles. Figure 2 shows an example of a flow-oriented model.

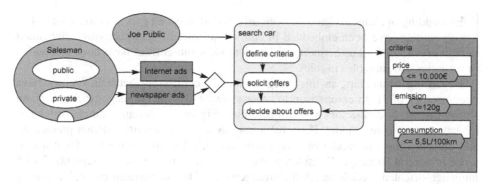

Fig. 2. Detail of a flow-oriented model example: "car selection of Joe Public" (translated from German to English by the authors)

Natural-Language-oriented Modeling Examples

This category covers models based on natural-language structures (subject-predicate-object). Overall, ten percent of the given models have been identified as language-oriented ones, i.e. 5 of 52 models.

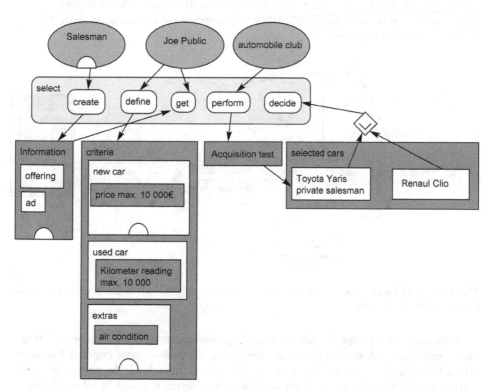

Fig. 3. Detail of a language-oriented model example: "car selection of Joe Public" (translated from German to English by the authors)

Embedding of elements has also been used within this category. In most cases (4 of 5) sub-entities have been embedded in entities, followed by sub-activities embedded in activities (3 of 5). Furthermore, in 2 of 5 models sub-entities have been embedded in activities and sub-roles in roles.

Regarding connectors, in this category mainly connectors between entities have been used (3 of 5). In comparison to other styles, only one language-oriented model shows the use of connectors between activities. Figure 3 gives an example of a natural-language-oriented model. Here, roles map to subjects, activities depict predicates, and entities represent model objects. Furthermore, relations are used to form a sentence in natural language. Considering the arrangement of the model elements, 2 of 5 language-oriented models match the arrangement of the subsequent example. Similar to the flow-oriented models, the remaining models show an arrangement of activities from top to bottom, with roles and entities aside.

Mixed Modeling Examples
Processes assigned to that category contain aspects from flow-, language-, or/and data-flow orientation. In our study 21 percent of the process models show such characteristics. An example is depicted in figure 4, which illustrates that the control flow between activities has not been modeled consistently within this category. Roles rather have been used to trigger activities, and entities have been used to model the data-flow between activities.

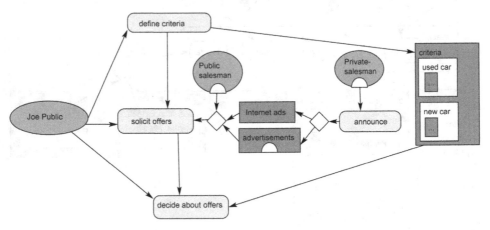

Fig. 4. Detail of a mixed model example: "car selection of Joe Public" (translated from German to English by the authors)

With respect to the applied SeeMe modeling constructs, the following observations have been made. Similar to the other categories, the embodiment concept has been utilized frequently (actually by 100 percent of the modelers). In particular, sub-activities and sub-entities have been embedded into super-activities in 10 of 11 cases. Furthermore, relating sub-roles to activities and sub-entities to super-entities could be observed in 6 out of 11 models. In 4 out of 11 models participants have represented sub-activities in entities and sub-roles in roles. Finally, sub-entities have been assigned to roles (in 3 out of 11 models).

The usage of connectors in this category matches with the other categories, again. 10 of 11 participants have used connectors. They have mainly used them to represent relations between entities (8 of 11 cases), followed by connectors between role-relations (7 cases) and connectors between activities (6 cases).

Process Specifications

The specified processes for purchasing a car show that all participants have used the basic elements of SeeMe to express "Who" does "What" "Using what". Furthermore all participants have applied relations between basic elements and constructs to express "Incompleteness". We have also identified the frequent utilization of the embodiment concept and the usage of connectors in the majority of cases. Thereby embedding has mainly been used to describe structural aspects of the given process, whereas connectors and relations have been used for depicting behavioral aspects.

The results reveal a strong orientation towards flow-oriented representations. Some modelers have mixed modeling approaches leading to inconsistencies with respect to styles and patterns. Besides flow orientation, SeeMe constructs have been used in a natural language style. In these cases, the reflection and reproduction of already speci-fied information could be achieved in complete sentences.

This variety of modeling patterns, resulting from using the identical core concepts of an open process-modeling language, shows that individual stakeholders assign different semantics to modeling constructs. It also shows their focus on different as-pects of processes.

Moreover, we have observed different arrangements of process elements and dif-ferent levels of detail. The majority of the modelers has depicted the concrete process of the given scenario and did not abstract to a general process of buying a car. How-ever, we have anticipated this result since the assignment did not explicitly address this instruction. We also assume the modelers had almost no experience in abstraction and modeling so far.

3.2 Discussion

Our results match the variety of today's process modeling notations and languages. Most of the modeling languages focus on flow-oriented representations rather than on natural language, or on a role-specific behavior specification. They rely on function-oriented flows of control for implementation. However, as Strosnider et al. [19] have found out recently, traditional flow-driven assembly and orchestration of (service) components are '*too rigid and static to accommodate complex, real-world business processes*' (p. 415). This finding indicates the demand for alternatives, even though our study reveals a strong orientation towards flow-driven modeling.

Our data provide evidence that natural language-based modeling could be consid-ered as an alternative modeling paradigm. Of particular interest seems to be the struc-ture (subject, predicate, and object) of natural language. Such an approach could help to bridge the gap between informal and formal representations, due to its capability to reduce the cognitive workload for specification. It could also facilitate focusing on relevant design elements of business processes. Future work will have to take into account previous knowledge of modelers with respect to modeling, e.g. experience with flowcharting or object-oriented modeling. It has to be studied whether inexperi-enced modelers use natural language structures rather than flow-oriented ones.

Although language can only be considered 'a window' into thoughts, as Pinker puts it [13], it offers the richest source of information about perceptual and cognitive processes. And, it is the most natural and comprehensive tool for communication, as people need to communicate for model building and information system development (cf. language-action perspective introduced by [22]). In fact, language structures might help to structure the perceived world, as recent empirical work in knowledge management reveals [21]. Based on hierarchical anchors, associations can be developed to represent information items and their situational context. Information spaces structured according to natural language constructs are partially compatible to existing business-process modeling techniques, such as ARIS [13], or JCOM1! [4]. The latter requires role or actor definitions being part of interactions to be performed for task accomplishment.

4 Conclusion

In our research we are looking for ways individuals are able to grasp the concept of business-process models and to develop modeling skills to participate actively in organizational change and (re-)engineering processes. In this paper we have presented the results of one of our studies on intuitive modeling. When designing and implementing the investigation we have tried to identify factors that cause confusion and prevent and the alignment of individual perspectives. In doing so, we were interested in finding constructs and a conceptual understanding of business processes allowing humans to represent knowledge about business process in an adequate way.

Students not familiar with modeling have been introduced to the idea of business-process modeling, and asked to model a car-purchasing scenario with a semi-structured notation. In the majority of cases individuals have focused on activities or functions to model relevant sub tasks along a certain sequence. The results, however, also indicate a bias towards natural language constructs besides mixed approaches.

We could identify various modeling patterns and styles. They reveal the individual assignment of semantics to modeling constructs, allowing individual emphasis of certain aspects when modeling processes. Hence, in order to achieve adequate representations of business processes, modelers need to be supported by constructs and representation schemes enabling them to articulate their individual mental representation. It could either be achieved by providing elements accounting for observed modeling paradigms, such as flow or natural-language orientation, or by semantically open modeling approaches. Mutual understanding and participatory change management seem to depend heavily on the means processes are represented and communicated.

Acknowledgments

The authors acknowledge Claudia Maderthaner for her editorial support.

We also would like to thank the participants of the study for their cooperative effort.

References

1. Brown, J., Duguid, P.: Organizing Knowledge. Reflections 1(2) (1999); Society of Organizational Learning
2. Fischer, H., Fleischmann, A., Obermeier, S.: Geschäftsprozesse realisieren. Vieweg, Wiesbaden (2006)
3. Fichtenbauer, C., Rumpfhuber, M., Stary, C.: Sprachgerechte unternehmensnahe Modellierung von ereignisgesteuerten Prozessketten – Zur adäquaten Aus- und Weiterbildung von ModelliererInnen. In: Proceedings EPK 2002, Workshop Ereignisgesteuerte Prozessketten, GI. Springer Lecture Notes, pp. 109–118 (2002)
4. Fleischmann, A.: Subjektorientiertes Geschäftsprozessmanagement, White Paper@ http://www.jcom1.com, jCOM1 AG, Rohrbach (2007)
5. Groff, T.R., Jones, T.P.: Introduction to Knowledge Management: Knowledge Management in Business. Butterworth/Heinemann, Amsterdam (2003)
6. Harel, D., Rumpe, B.: Meaningful Modeling: What's the semantics of "Semantics"? IEEE Computer 37(10), 64–72 (2004)
7. Havey, M.: Essential Business Process Modelling. O'Reilly, Sebastopol (2005)
8. Haeckel, S.H.: Adaptive enterprise: Creating and leading sense-AND-respond organizations. Harvard Business School Press, Cambridge (1999)
9. Herrmann, T., Loser, K.-U.: Vagueness in models of socio-technical systems. Behaviour and Information Technology 18(5), 313–323 (1999)
10. Herrmann, T.: SeeMe in a nutshell – the semi-structured, socio-technical modeling method (2006),
http://www.imtm-iaw.rub.de/imperia/md/content/seeme/
seeme_in_a_nutshell.pdf
11. Jørgensen, H.: Interactive Process Models. PhD thesis, Department of Computer and Information Sciences, Norwegian University of Science and Technology Trondheim (2004)
12. Lewis, M., Young, B., Mathiassen, L., Rai, A., Welke, R.: Business process innovation based on stakeholder perceptions. Information Knowledge Systems Management 6, 7–17 (2007)
13. Pinker, S.: The Stuff of thought: Language as a window into human nature. Allen Lane, London (2007)
14. Rouse, W.B. (ed.): Enterprise transformation: Understanding and enabling fundamental change. Wiley, Hoboken (2006)
15. Sarini, M., Simone, C.: Recursive articulation work in Ariadne: The alignment of meanings. In: Proceedings of COOP 2002, pp. 191–206 (2002)
16. Scheer, A.-W.: ARIS - Modellierungsmethoden, Metamodelle, Anwendungen, 4th edn. Springer, Berlin (2002)
17. Scheer, A.W., Kruppke, H., Jost, W., Kindermann, H. (eds.): Agilität durch ARIS-Geschäftsprozessmanagement. Jahrbuch Business Process Excellence 2006/2007. Springer, Berlin (2006)
18. Seidelmeier, H.: Prozessmodellierung mit ARIS®. Eine beispielorientierte Einführung für Studium und Praxis. Vieweg, Wiesbaden (2002)
19. Strosnider, J.K., Nandi, P., Kumaran, S., Ghosh, S., Arsanjani, A.: Model-driven synthesis of SOA solutions. IBM Systems Journal 41(5), 415–432 (2008)
20. Weick, K.E.: The social psychology of organizations. Addison Wesley, Reading (1999)
21. Wieden, W.: Corporate linguistics: A knowledge management approach to language. AAA - Arbeiten aus Anglistik und Amerikanistik 31(2), 185–207 (2006)
22. Winograd, T.: A language/action perspective on the design of collaborative work. In: Greif, I. (ed.) Computer-Supported Cooperative Work. A Book of Readings, pp. 623–653. Morgan Kaufman, San Mateo (1988)

Supporting Business Model Modelling: A Compromise between Creativity and Constraints

Boris Fritscher and Yves Pigneur

University of Lausanne, 1015 Lausanne, Switzerland
boris.fritscher@unil.ch, yves.pigneur@unil.ch

Abstract. Diagrams and tools help to support task modelling in engineering and process management. Unfortunately they are unfit to help in a business context at a strategic level, because of the flexibility needed for creative thinking and user friendly interactions. We propose a tool which bridges the gap between freedom of actions, encouraging creativity, and constraints, allowing validation and advanced features.

1 Introduction

Representing information and tasks has gained importance at all levels: UML class diagrams, CAD, business process modelling, GDSS, at nearly every stage there are models to help us cope with the complexity of structuring information. Business information management at a strategic level is not an exception to it, but contrary to the other fields it lacks the visual tools to support them. The problem is in part due to the business objects which have no real fixed representation that can be formalized by a specification, and also due to the freedom needed in such models to allow a creative thinking process. These requirements make it difficult to utilize the more classical task modelling tools which have more strict representation of their objects.

For a tool to support an application in the business context, the challenge is to provide enough specialized functionality to enforce the rules of the methodology (meta-model), without compromising the freedom of creativity. This creativity is the necessary intuition for abstracting the business model to a strategic level out of ongoing activities. From a research methodology standpoint we decided to adopt Hevner et al's design science research framework[1], which focuses on solving a real world problem by applying knowledge to an information system prototype conceived iteratively. Therefore, we focused on resolving the gap between creativity and constraints by creating a new tool. This software has to at the same time, be as flexible as a paper based method, but in addition shares features with computer assisted design programmes. This paper explores the compromises which were required and demonstrate the resulting prototype.

First we introduce the business model canvas we choose to support. Then we review some of the existing models and their support tools. In the third section we present the tool and its iterations. We then discuss some of the early testing which was done. In the last section we look at future iterations of the proposed visual tool.

D. England et al. (Eds.): TAMODIA 2009, LNCS 5963, pp. 28–43, 2010.

2   Designing Business Models

2.1   Business Model Canvas

For our prototype we choose to implement a tool for a very visual business model canvas called the Business Model Ontology[2]. A business model canvas or ontology (BMO) can be described by looking at a set of nine building blocks. These building blocks were derived from an in-depth literature review of a large number of previous conceptualizations of business models. In this depiction, the business model of a company is a simplified representation of its business logic viewed from a strategic standpoint (i.e. on top of Business Process Modelling). The layout of the nine component has its importance as can be seen in figure 1.

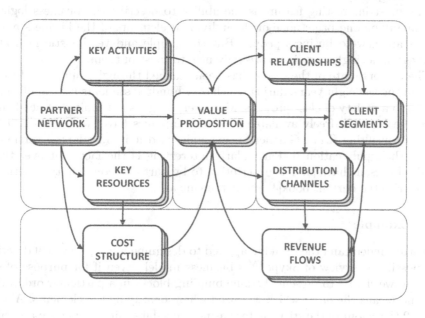

Fig. 1. Business Model Ontology Canvas

Each building block can contain elements instantiating the building block's business logic. For example, *Customer Segments* could be teenagers, families, young single men. Every element is represented by a sticky note in the real world or a distinctively identifiable component in a digital representation.

At the centre there is the *Value Proposition*, it describes which customer's problems are solved and why the offer is more valuable than similar products from competitors (product, service). The customer themselves are analysed in *Customer Segment*, separated into groups to help in identifying their needs, desires and ambitions (singles, families). *Distribution Channel* illustrates how the customer wants to be reached and by whom he is addressed (Internet, store). In addition, *Customer Relationships* specifies what type of relationship the customer expects and how it is establish and maintained with him (promotion, support, individual or mass). To be able to deliverer the value proposition the business has to have *Resources* (staff, machines, secret knowledge). And transform theses resources through *Key Activities* into the final product or service (development, production, secret process). Most of the time a business depends also either for resources or for activities on an external *Partner Network* (logistics, financial), which can provide better quality or a lower price on non essential components. As any business model would not be complete without financial information the last two building blocks focus on cost and revenue: The *Cost Structure* which should be aligned to the core ideas of the business model (key resources, key activities) and *Revenue Streams* which mirrors the value the customers are willing to pay an how they will perform the transaction (one time fee, subscription).

The most interesting feature is the ability to describe the business logic of a company on one page: none of the individual elements of the business model canvas are new to business people. But the simple and yet holistic look at a business on a single page is surprisingly new to most of them.

The current state of the canvas has been reached through a number of iterations in the last eight years, during which over hundred students have applied the canvas to a variety of class projects. Moreover, usage is not limited to academia; since the model is freely available a lot of companies have started using it, as well as consulting firms. Gartner for example used it in an adapted version in one of their publication[3]. Particularly interesting is the fact that over three hundred persons have paid a subscription to be part of a community experience to co-write the current book[4] about the canvas.

2.2 Example

To better understand the thinking applied to designing a model, we will describe one possible overview of Skype^{TM}'s business model. Even if for purpose of explaining we choose to present the nine building blocks in a particular order, this is by no means the order which was used when identifying the elements. Also in figure 2 the colour of the sticky notes has no special meaning. Skype's main value proposition is to offer free VoIP & video calling. In addition, they offer additional services like for example cheap international calls through Skype out. Their customer segments are mainly global mass customers and they also try to target SMEs. To be able to reach their customers Skype uses the internet to distribute their software, but they also bundle a cdrom of their application with some of Logitech^{TM}'s webcams. Support of their service is also done through their internet website to allow for mass customization. Since the software and the basic service are offered for free, we show the importance of this fact by adding a sticky note called free to revenue streams. The other real revenues are from their bundle agreements and the Skype out charges. Service usage having been described, we focus on how the value proposition is produced. The resources which Skype needs to provide their service is their software and the software developers building it. These resources are used in an activity of software development. In addition, Skype has to maintain an activity of fraud management using for

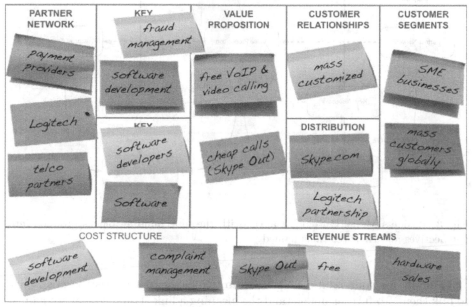

Fig. 2. Skype's Business Model

resources their staff and partners. Skype is heavily dependent on their partners since, they do not have their own network infrastructure. Therefore, they need payment providers, telecommunication providers, and naturally hardware vendor. Finally, everything has a cost, but it was decided to feature software development and complaint management as the main cost structures.

2.3 Business Model Ontology

The canvas shown in figure 1 is a simplified version of the real business model ontology canvas in order to facilitate working with it. The real canvas of the BMO meta-model is depicted in figure 3 and adds perspectives and links to the building blocks.

When describing the example there already emerges a way to group some building blocks together. We propose to call theses groupings perspectives. As can be seen in figure 3 we identify four perspectives. The value proposition is in its own perspective. Financial aspects like cost and revenue have been grouped into a financial perspective. Moreover, the remaining six blocks have been split into two perspectives: activity and customer. They both are somewhat mirrored, due to the specific position in the canvas. The activity perspective focuses on how the value proposition is produced and the customer perspective how it is consumed.

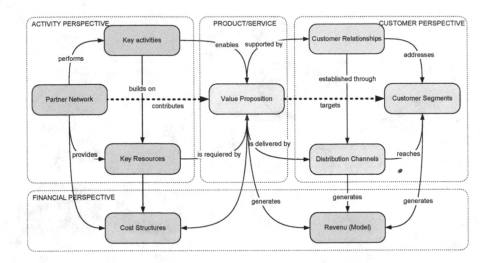

Fig. 3. Business Model Ontology Canvas with the nine building blocks grouped into perspectives and their relations named

To imply a strong relationship between two elements there is the possibility to link them. To further understand the meaning a link should convey we named them in figure 3. For example, applied to Skype's canvas: free VoIP targets mass customers, which are reached by skype.com delivering it. This way of connecting the elements can also help in identifying missing elements in neighbouring blocks.

2.4   Typical Session

To better understand the BMO methodology let us describe the tasks involved in a paper based session. The power of the method originates from its visual positioning of the block and the relationship they have between each other. Simply adding, removing or changing sticky notes containing a short title, to the building blocks, helps in identifying existing business models, as well as new opportunities. The typical setting is to work on a whiteboard or a big piece of paper, depending on the number of users. The preparation work is to draw an empty canvas on the working surface. After that, the user can start to add an element to any building block, or even temporarily store a sticky note with his idea on a border. As the elements are on sticky notes they can easily be moved, grouped or discarded. If there is a strong relationship between some elements a link will be drawn between them. Elements can be grouped together or even be replaced by a more generalized element during the creation process, or elements can be refined and become a new sticky note. After an initial brainstorm, it can be useful to focus on a specific perspective and identify the strong links between elements and see if there are some missing components.

2.5   Technique and Task

There are no given task sequences to follow in order to design a business model with the Business Model Canvas[4]. An element (sticky note) can be added at one place and then moved or even removed. The important thing is the discussion it generated, and perhaps the other elements which have been identified through this discussion. Therefore, instead of identifying small task which can be executed in an undefined order or repeated, we instead propose some techniques to help structure the idea generation without imposing a too formal process. These techniques include, but are not limited to: *Brainstorming*[5], *ideation, visual thinking, customer insight, storytelling, scenarios*[4].

In general, it is a good practice to generate ideas by adding everything we think of to the canvas. Like in a *Brainstorming* session, the ideas have to be written down without jugging them. Some persons are more inspired by visuals; this can be addressed by drawing a *sketch* of an object illustrating the element that has to be added. The drawn object does not need to be a perfect representation of the element, but can also be a *metaphor* of the activity. A small illustration can communicate a lot more than a single word. Naturally, at some point the *visuals* will have to be describes by a text clearly sharing its full meaning and the amount of generated elements through creative *thinking* will have to be synthesised into a coherent working business model. Perspectives, besides helping to group the nine blocks into fewer components, can be interesting starting points. A business model can have its focus centred on the resources (activity perspective), the value proposition itself, the customer or even focus on the financials at the very beginning. Once the canvas is already populated with elements, it can be helpful to see which element is linked to others. This identifies if an element is missing, another way to get more related elements is to use *storytelling*. Telling a story involving the elements and how they are connected, can not only show missing or unused elements, but helps in communicating the whole business model to outsiders. The business canvas covers different knowledge area about a company; it is therefore natural that the design activity should be performed in *groups*, discussing the opinions of each other. The task of *co-designing* is very important, since every participant has to be aware that his vision is not the only one and should be able to take the stakeholder's perspective about the element which is discussed.

2.6   Life Cycle

In its current state the business model canvas[4] and the application supporting it consider a completed canvas as the finished product itself. The business model components are not transformed to generate a process, but the canvas as a whole provides a map or an overview for the management of the current service offering, or a future offering, they aspire to reach. Even though, the canvas can be used at different stage of a business model lifecycle and could in future work be extend to be used as a reference for implementing appropriate solution in other tools.

Process

- *Mobilize* people to generate new business opportunities: in this first phase the business model canvas can help to set a simple common language through its nine blocks, links and layout.
- *Understand* the current situation: using the above described techniques the canvas helps to regroup the collected information and hints at missing information.
- *Design*, extending the business model: with the sticky notes and it all in one page format, alternatives can be identified until a best one emerges.
- *Implement* the chosen business model: the canvas and techniques like story telling help share the vision and therefore facilitated the implementation.
- *Manage* the current business model: like strategy maps the canvas could help to monitor the current situation.

In its paper form, the final designed business model canvas is shared as a picture of the sticky notes, or for better sharing it is sometimes recreated in a time consuming task on a graphics program. The biggest drawback of these representations is that they lack any additional semantic value. In the next section we take a look at other visual methodologies and how their tools have tried to overcome this problem.

3   Overview of Tools Assisting Design

Most of the time innovation starts on a piece of paper, as a little sketch or some keywords which are written on it. This is done mostly to structure ideas, remember them or help communicate them. Communicating one's ideas can generate discussions and help us generate new ones. In addition, the paper represents the shared knowledge, as well as the history of the collaboration session. Today, there are many techniques to help strengthen the power of manual note taking. Some are best used in a multi-user scenario like Brainstorming[5], while others are intended for a single user like some note taking canvas. The constraints of these techniques can be very structured like in said canvas or unstructured like in Brainstorming which really insist on pushing the boundaries of creativity with its rules. There are also techniques which are semi-structured and can be used as well in a single user, as in a multi-user context, like Mind Maps[6] and concept maps[7].

Many tools exist to support these techniques, but they are all lacking some features to be really useful in a business modelling context. The more unstructured tools like Mind maps provide a great range of freedom to create elements as ideas come to mind, but lack the possibility to impose meta-model constraints. Structured tools, like CAD programs, are for the major part very feature reach, but always geared towards a specific domain. This makes them very powerful for the expert user, but useless for office workers. Furthermore, their complexity often requires a sequential input which hinders creative thinking[8]. For example, Protégé is a powerful ontology editor, but is hard to use by a novice user to simply navigate or add his custom element.

The key is to find the right balance between supporting the model by enforcing its rules and still give the user enough degrees of freedom to allow him to follow his own path of creation. The application should be flexible enough to allow for its interaction to be as semless and close as possible to the paper based version and still enforce the meta-model's constraints to be able to provide additional value.

For example, Consideo-modeler[1] is a nice solution which implements a complete workflow from strategy level modelling down to process level with simulation possibilities, but it requires having quite a lot of knowledge about their modelling rules and there are advanced dialogs boxes to configure the required attributes. A lot more intuitive, Lombardi's BluePrint[2] web offering allows for real-time collaborative process modelling design. Their service is a good example of collaborative application done with web technologies, but a process model is a lot more structured than the business model canvas we propose to use. On the other hand a tool like Denim[9] offers great capabilities of zoom levels and ways to create and explore hierarchical content, but through their blank canvas do not provide the block constraint needed to have a meta-model which is stronger than just links. Outpost[10] which has an interesting tangile approach towards sticky notes, suffers from the same problem where the importance is set on the link and not the position. Sketchixml[11] shows how we can forgo the need to create elements before using them by drawing their content directly. Is also proposes direct design feedback through pattern analyse, but is geared towards user interface design.

No tool having all the necessary features of constraint versus freedom we required, we propose our own implementation of a solution meeting our need.

4   Specification of the Design Artefact

The initial goal for our prototype was to replicate the sticky note experience of adding, moving and discarding elements in the most natural and intuitive way to users, used to the paper based experience. The goal is not only to mimic the user's interaction experience, but also the way the canvas' possibilities drive the creative session. Thus, keeping the trial and error aspect of paper based sticky notes is a core design choice we made throughout the project.

4.1   Prototypes

In the current iteration of the prototype, a *double click* creates a new element and *drag and drop* moves it (figure 4). Discarding an element is done by replicating a trashcan; drop an element on it to remove it. The intention is to provide a feeling as close as possible to the real world sticky note experience. But the fact that the elements now are digital, allows for new functionalities, like giving elements some attributes which can be used to better describe them. We also added a possibility to store annotations to keep track of design choices or ideas for future changes.

---

[1] http://www.consideo-modeler.de/
[2] http://www.lombardisoftware.com/

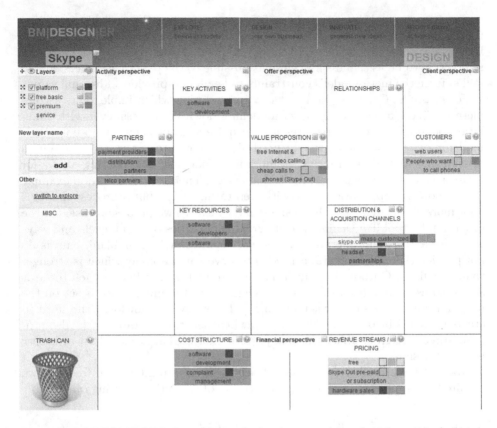

Fig. 4. *BM|DESIGN|ER* design view: dragging *mass customized* from relationships to distribution channels

Some degrees of freedom of drag and drop operations have been limited to allow only movement between the nine blocks, this to ensure that the meta-model of the canvas is maintained. This and element's attributes gives the virtual canvas a semantic meaning which can contributes to more advanced features.

We have created multiple prototypes and iterations[12], but to a certain level they share all the same set of basic interaction features, as well as the ability to link elements (by drag and dropping one element over another). Moreover, a layer feature has also been added. An element can belong to one or more layers and each layer can be turned on or off. For example, a layer identified by a specific colour can be used for each product offering thereby helping to identify which other elements are used by multiple products and thus very important for the business. Different layers can also be used to identify alternatives or future evolutions of the business model.

The concept of versioning has been extended in one of the prototype (figure 5) to allow for taking snapshots (saving its states) and drawing a graph of the history of snapshots of a model. From each snapshot a new branch can be created. This was extended to a notion of merging, by adding multiple instances

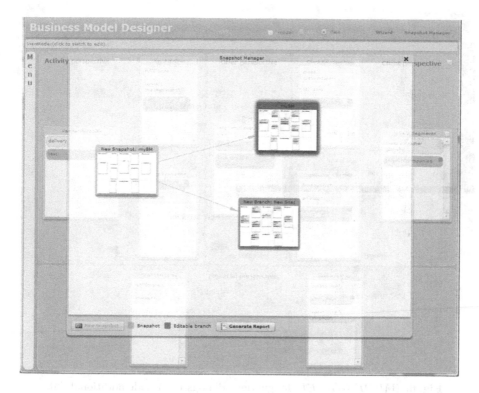

Fig. 5. Flex prototype: overview of snapshots (versions) of a Business Model

of a model onto a separate layer of a new empty canvas, thus enabling a limited comparison of the merged business models.

To further enhance the usefulness of the digital application we tested the notion of wizard, which would guide the user through some question to help him identify missing elements. This is intended to be used after the initial creative thinking process since using it at the beginning would render our tool very structured and thereby missing our initial intention.

The last version of our prototype called $BM|DESIGN|ER$ [3] focuses more on ways to navigate through created business models and collaborating on new business model ideas with the help of a community. This is achieved by having a website with modern social web interactions: commenting, voting, tagging, categorizing and searching.

4.2 Example

To better illustrate the prototype and its interaction techniques the Skype example was reproduced on $BM|DESIGN|ER$ [4] and are described with the help

---

[3] http://bmdesigner.com

[4] http://bmdesigner.com/explore/bm/67/Skype

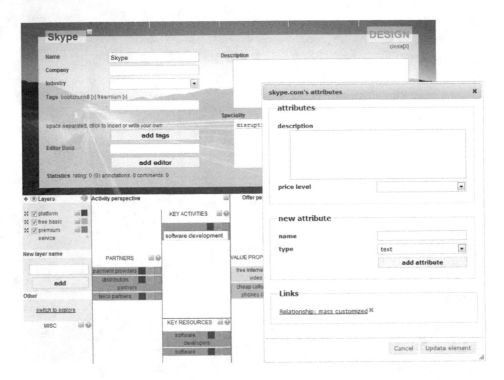

Fig. 6. *BM|DESIGN|ER* design view: dialogs to provide additional data

of figures 4, 6, 7. When creating a new business model the canvas is empty. By double-clicking one of the nine building blocks the user can add a new element (virtual sticky note) to it through an input dialog box which asks for the element's name. Once it is created it is possible to provide additional attributes. This can be seen in the right hand side of figure 6. Some default attributes are provided for each element type, but new ones can be configured at the user's discretion. Figure 6 also illustrates the input box displayed when clicking an element to rename it (look for the software development element), as well as additional attributes which can be added at the canvas level like tags (top part of the figure). Figure 4 illustrates the drag and drop behaviours. An element can be dragged to a different building block, here *mass customized* is moved from *relationships* to *distribution channel*. While dragging new possible positions for the currently dragged element are highlighted to the user by an empty element at the open spot. The possibility to link two elements is shown when dragging one element over another, the element which is not dragged has its appearance changed (red border and background). Upon releasing an element in a link creation action, the dragged element will go back to its original position, but both elements will have been linked.

In the example shown in figure 4, three layers have been define to make out the free versus premium service Skype offers, and the elements which both these service depend on (platform). Layers are created with the left hand side menu.

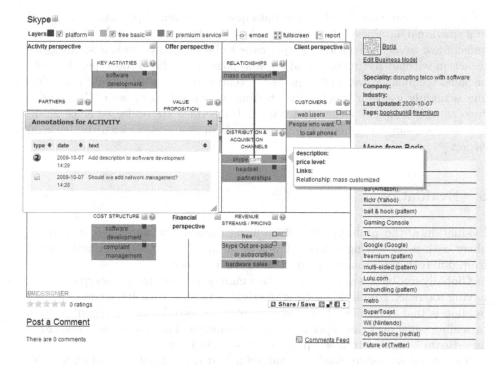

Fig. 7. *BM|DESIGN|ER* explore view: displaying links and reading annotations

Adding and removing an element to a layer is done by toggling the corresponding colour swatch on each element. The small sticky note icon which can be seen next to each layer and building block title bring up a dialog to add annotations. Annotations can also have priorities to behave like to-do tasks. In the case of to-do's, the type of annotation shows a number related to its priority. Figure 7 shows annotations of the key activity block from a viewer's angle. The two first figures showed the edition mode (design) of the prototype, while this third one shows the guest mode (explore). In this mode double-clicking an element will draw links it has with other elements. The link between *mass customized* and *skype.com* can be seen in figure 7. In view mode the user cannot add new annotations, but he can post comments at the bottom of the canvas, as well as rate it.

4.3   Implementation

The prototype is developed on the Grails[5] framework to capitalize on modern features like convention over coding, Model View Controller and Object Relational Mapping that these web frameworks provide. In addition, Grails has the advantage of being able to use a lot of third party libraries since it run on the java runtime environment. Therefore, by convention the architectzre is separated into

---

[5] http://grails.org/

data and presentation. The backend data manipulation and persistence is stored in a relational database. The frontend is built in standard web technologies with quiet a few asynchronous JavaScript[6] calls to be able to provide a seamless interaction without having to reload the web page. In a prior prototype, the same backend technology was used, but the frontend was design in Adobe Flex[7]. This one is mainly used for touch device testing, which still presents challenging in current web browsers. Other than that web interface are preferred since modifications are simpler, loading time faster and communication with the backend easier.

5   Evaluation

Evaluation of the prototype was done using cognitive walkthrough[7] methodology with users having different levels of familiarity of the BMO and coming from different backgrounds (students and businessmen).

Globally feedback was positive. Testers managed to use the prototype without having too much trouble identifying the right action for their intensions. General opinion is that versioning, layers and annotation features may certainly help in providing value over the paper based static solution. There was also a test using an e-Beam [8] touch screen setup as can be seen in figure 8.

The idea was twofold: firstly, we wanted to test usability of the tool with a wall projected solution; secondly, we were interested to compare on-screen interaction to the paper based system in relation to group interactions, brainstorming possibilities and other design aspects. We will continue investigating applicability of the tool in a collaborative context, in future iterations, as during preliminary testing mostly usability problems were detected.

As for the business model community testing site, we just started, but already has over 200 users and 150 models including all the business models from an upcoming book. We hope to be able to study real interaction usage through logs of our tool and use the community as testing platform for new features.

In terms of evaluation, we only are at the beginning and still have a lot of ground to cover. There is an additional difficulty, that in some cases, it is hard to distinguish between problems originating in lack of usability, or in lack of understanding of the business model canvas methodology. For example, do users prefer to use annotations instead of virtual sticky notes because of usability, or methodology? Or even, because on the current prototype all business models are public, due to concerns for the privacy of their model. Either they are generally cautious about their ideas, or this could indicate that even if there are only keywords on the canvas, the users feel it provides enough insight into their activity that it warrants protection. This could be interpreted as an indicatin to the usefulness of the canvas' expressive power.

---

[6] http://jquery.com/

[7] http://www.adobe.com/products/flex/

[8] http://e-beam.com/

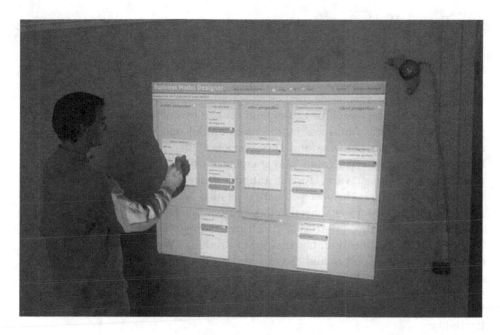

Fig. 8. Prototype projected onto a wall and eBeam interact as pointer

6   Discussion and Conclusion

Our research has been conducted according to Hevner et al's design science research framework[1] and has fulfilled the requirements of his proposed seven guidelines.

1. *Design as an Artifact*: we developed prototypes which can be evaluated.
2. *Problem Relevance*: we have shown that a tool supporting business model innovation is relevant and emerges from a real business need.
3. *Design Evaluation*: Preliminary evaluation results suggest that the proposed solution is useful in helping to overcome barriers between creativity of business model innovation and constraints of modelling tools.
4. *Research Contributions*: we contributed to the business model ontology by refining links between the elements.
5. *Research Rigor*: the business model canvas we based our research on has been validated and is itself based on known ontology research.
6. *Design as a Search Process*: we iteratively built several prototypes based on evaluation feedback.
7. *Communication of Research*: Earlier prototypes have been presented in a Master Thesis as well as a workshop on modelling (VMBO 2009, Stockholm).

We have shown that it is possible to find a compromise between freedom and constraints to keep idea generation going, but still enforce a meta-model. Digital alternatives to paper based methodologies can help in providing additional value and style be user friendly enough to be used by office worker.

6.1   Future Work

We hope to grow a community around our tool to promote business model innovation at a strategic level and collect valuable feedback. Some tests have been done to investigate collaboration possibility which can be offered by tabletops or touch walls, but this needs further research

There are many possibilities to extend on the prototype as well from an hci perspective as from a business model meta-model one. For example, selective zoom and focus on elements and their details depending on the context, like is done in Denim[9]. We could also imagine moving from a sketch level to a more detailed element view. Testing tangible interactions with real stick notes likes was done in the Outpost project[10] is also an interesting opportunity to further explore ways to enhanced collaboration as well as bridging information and usability. Another interesting direction to explore is to try some kind of SketchiXML[11] application, but instead of drawing UI-elements the user would draw business components and directly generate an appropriate XML or OWL description of the business model. In relation to the stages of the business model canvas' lifecycle, it would also make sense to explore the possibilities offered by multi-fidelity user interfaces[13] to better fit the stage's different needs of flexibility.

As for extending the business model such a tool would benefit of being more than a tool to help designing the model, but also manage the active version by helping at monitoring it like a dashboard. Such a tool could also help in identifing future or alternative version of business model by providing simulation possibilities.

References

1. Hevner, A.R., March, S.T., Park, J., Ram, S.: Design science in information systems research. Management Information Systems Quarterly 28(1), 75–105 (2004)
2. Osterwalder, A., Pigneur, Y.: An e-business model ontology for modeling e-business. In: 15th Bled Electronic Commerce Conference, Bled, Slovenia, pp. 17–19 (2002)
3. Gartner: Getting the right IT: using business models. EXP CIO signature (October 2007)
4. Osterwalder, A., Pigneur, Y.: Business Model Generation. businessmodelgeneration.com (2009)
5. Osborn, A.F.: Applied Imagination: Principles and Procedures of Creative Problem-Solving, 3rd rev. edn. Creative Education Foundation (February 1993)
6. Buzan, T.: The mind map book: how to use radiant thinking to maximize your brain's untapped potential. Plume, New York (1993)
7. Novak, J.D., Canas, A.J.: The theory underlying concept maps and how to construct them. University of West Florida (2001)
8. Stacey, M., Eckert, C.: CAD system bias in engineering design. In: Proceedings of the 12th International Conference on Engineering Design, vol. 2, pp. 923–928 (1999)

9. Lin, J., Newman, M.W., Hong, J.I., Landay, J.A.: DENIM: finding a tighter fit between tools and practice for web site design. In: Proceedings of the SIGCHI conference on Human factors in computing systems, pp. 510–517. ACM, New York (2000)
10. Klemmer, S.R., Newman, M.W., Farrell, R., Bilezikjian, M., Landay, J.A.: The designers' outpost: a tangible interface for collaborative web site. In: Proceedings of the 14th annual ACM symposium on User interface software and technology, pp. 1–10. ACM, New York (2001)
11. Coyette, A., Faulkner, S., Kolp, M., Limbourg, Q., Vanderdonckt, J.: SketchiXML: towards a Multi-Agent design tool for sketching user interfaces based on UsiXML. In: Proc. of 3rd Int. Workshop on Task Models and Diagrams for user interface design, TAMODIA 2004, pp. 75–82. ACM, New York (2004)
12. Fritscher, B.: Business Model Designer From Post-it to screen interaction. Ms, University of Lausanne (December 2008)
13. Memmel, T., Vanderdonckt, J., Reiterer, H.: Multi-fidelity user interface specifications. In: Graham, T.C.N., Palanque, P. (eds.) DSV-IS 2008. LNCS, vol. 5136, pp. 43–57. Springer, Heidelberg (2008)

A Service-Oriented Approach for Interactive System Design

Jorge Luis Pérez Medina, Sophie Dupuy-Chessa, and Dominique Rieu

University of Grenoble, CNRS, LIG
385 rue de la Bibliothèque, BP 53
F-38041 GRENOBLE cedex 9, France
{Jorge-Luis.Perez-Medina,Sophie.Dupuy,Dominique.Rieu}@imag.fr

Abstract. The introduction of new technologies leads to a more and more complex interactive systems design. In order to describe the future interactive system, the human computer interaction domain uses specific models, design processes and tools in order to represent, create, store and manipulate models. The aim of our work is to facilitate the work of model designers and project managers by helping them in choosing processes, modeling environments adapted to their specific needs. This paper details the use of a service-oriented approach for model management. Our propositions are related to three different abstract levels: the operational level to choose the appropriate tool, the organisational level to select a process and the intentional level to define modelling goals.

Keywords: HCI, model, service, model management, modeling tools, modeling services.

1 Introduction

In the Human Computer Interaction (HCI) domain, interactive systems are increasingly complex: they can use everyday life objects to propose tangible interfaces; they can couple the virtual and the physical worlds in augmented reality systems; they can adapt themselves to the user context, etc. Then they are increasingly difficult to design.

The HCI community made many proposals to address this design complexity. Some of them are based on ad-hoc code centric approaches, while others use usability properties (as the ISO/IEC 9126[1]) or ergonomic requirements [1], [2] [27], in order to make user interfaces (UIs) more usable. These recommendations refer to ergonomic properties (as usefulness, users experience, etc.) that often cannot be formalizes as process and models, because they may contain a part of subjective appreciations.

On the other hand, substantive efforts have been devoted to the definition and use of models, and extensive development of software support has been achieved. We are interested in those propositions that are based on models.

The HCI community uses different models to support the design of interactive systems. In particular, the HCI design is often based on task analysis, which is classically

---

[1] The ISO/IEC 9126 series are part of the stands defined by the software engineering community for the standardization of "quality of use" on a software product.

D. England et al. (Eds.): TAMODIA 2009, LNCS 5963, pp. 44–57, 2010.
© Springer-Verlag Berlin Heidelberg 2010

represented by task trees. Moreover the use of these models can be guided by specific processes. Many interactive system design methods have been proposed. They are often based on task analysis [22], [28], [30]. Many efforts are also related to contextual design [4], [11], scenario-based approaches [8], [25] and iterative prototyping [14].

The choice of such processes is a strategic decision carried out considering the goals expected by the model designers. For example, in the HCI domain, the Human is the most important aspect in all phases of the development process. For consequent, a modeling goal is the "study the user interaction". During this study, the designer can discover that instead of a classical WIMP interface, the design of a mixed reality system is more appropriate. So he will have a new goal "design a mixed reality system" for which he needs a specific process. Therefore, a rigid method is no longer desired and there is a need to support method definition and adaptation.

To face these needs of adaptation and flexibility in the design, we propose to help model designers and project managers in choosing processes according to their modeling goals. For example, based on the goal "study the user interaction", a model designer will be able to choose the methods of fragments of processes, such as the Organizational and Interactional Specifications of Requirements of the Symphony method [9] or the Elaboration phase of the extended RUP proposed by [16].

The choice of a process determines the models to use, and then their modeling environments. For instance, selecting the process proposed to design an Interactive system give rise to use of the ConcurTaskTrees (CTT) notation and then to the choice of CTTE [19] for its support.

Our approach is based on the reuse of existing processes and technological solutions in order to find solution to the goals of designers and managers. It concerns the adaptation of Service Oriented Architecture (SOA) [18] to model management. It is based on three abstract levels: the operational level, the organizational level and the intentional level: 1) operational services carry out automated operations (e.g. editing a model); 2) organizational services propose fragments of design methods i.e. processes; 3) the intentional services correspond to the goals proposed by any person or organization handling models. This paper focuses on the intentional and the organization levels which are the main contributions of our work.

This paper is organized as follows. Section 2 describes two experimental scenarios. These examples are based on interactive system design methods. Section 3 presents our approach based on service-oriented models management. Sections 4 and 5 detail the models of the intentional and organizational layers. Section 6 presents a platform support for our service-oriented approach. Finally, conclusions and perspectives are presented.

2 Interactive Design Method

The scope of our study is not situated in the choice of ideal interactive system design methods. We aim at the choice of appropriate processes and modeling tools. To explain our approach, we focus on two interactive system design methods. Our goal is to demonstrate how our service-oriented approach can support the construction of modeling environment used for interactive system design.

The first method is an extension of the Symphony design method [13], used as a medium for merging HCI and software engineering development processes. Symphony is a user-oriented, business component-based development method originally proposed by the UMANIS Company. It has been extended lately to integrate the design of Augmented Reality systems [9].

In this article, we concentrate on the phase of the "Organizational and Interactional Specifications of Requirements" (Figure 1). This phase aims to analyze a business process at organizational level (the "who does what and when" of the future system), and to envisage a satisfactory interaction to realize activities of different stakeholders.

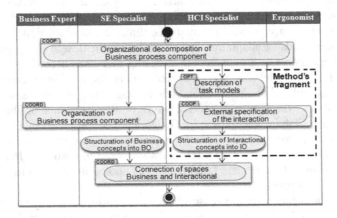

Fig. 1. A phase of the Symphony method [9]

Concerning the HCI aspects (box of Figure 1), the activities proposed by the design method are: **description of task models** to clarify the interactions of the internal actors with the system, **external specification of the interaction** to define the user interface (UI) and its supporting devices, and **Structuration of Interaction concepts into a specific model** composed of reusable components **called Interactional Objects (IO)**. These actions must be driven by the ergonomics and the HCI specialist.

The second approach [29] used for model-based design of user interfaces. It is founded on the Cameleon Reference Framework [7]. The approach allows designers defining a model-based user interface development (UID) method according to the problem domain or context of the project by analyzing goals and activities. It is composed of four-step reification process: 1) create conceptual models (e.g. task model, data model, user model) which bring the descriptions produced by the designers for that particular interactive system and that particular context of use; 2) create Abstract UI (AUI) which specify objects in a UI independent of device, create Concrete UI (CUI) which makes explicit the final look and feel of the Final User Interface considering device constraints, and create Final UI (FUI) which is expressed in source code.

Figure 2 illustrates a global vision of this process. Concerning the HCI aspects of the Usability Expert, the activities proposed by the design method are: **Create Context of Use Model** to design user-centered UIs, **Create AUI** to specify objects in a UI independent from devices, **Transform into Task Model** to automate the generation

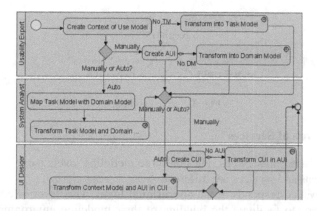

Fig. 2. An interactive system modeling process [29]

of specification of UIs (receive AUI as input and generate task model), and finally **Transform into Domain Model** to automate the generation of UIs focused on the application domain for describing the manipulated data.

In the remainder of this paper, these two examples are used to illustrate our approach for model management.

3   General Approach

3.1   Introduction

This section proposes the concepts of our service-oriented approach for models management with services. In our approach, modeling services enables to structure the set of knowledge which is necessary to the description of goals, in order to facilitate and to automate software development steps using models (e.g. model edition, model transformation, etc).

3.2   The Basic Service-Oriented Architecture

Service-Oriented Computing (SOC) is a paradigm that uses services as fundamental elements for developing applications [17]. This development approach speeds the application development and facilitates the composition of distributed applications. A service is a set of self-contained software modules and auto-descriptive applications that can be described, published, discovered, composed, and negotiated on demand by a customer. **Services** perform functions, which can be anything from simple requests to complicated business processes [18]. This approach defines an interaction between software agents as an exchange of messages between service requesters (customers) and service providers (Figure 3). **Customers** are software agents that request the execution of a service. Customers must be able to find the description(s) of the services they require and must be able to bind them. **Providers** are software agents that provide the service. Agents can be simultaneously service customers and providers. Providers are responsible for publishing a description of the service(s) they provide.

Fig. 3. Service approach

3.3 Three Levels of Services

Our approach based on services relies on three modeling levels (see Figure 4) where providers, clients and services are different.

The first level corresponds to the **operational layer**. This layer offers services for model designers, to facilitate the building of their modeling environment. The customers are designers who want to manage models in an individual or collaborative way (with other designers). So, they should define and adjust their modeling environment to theirs needed functions in terms of models management. For example: an "HCI designer" can need a modeling environment that offers support for editing "task models" and transforming these models into a "concrete user interface" (CUI) for a specific device.

The organizational layer decomposes information system development methods as fragments. Several types of fragments have emerged in the literature. The most known of these different kind of representation are method fragments [6], chunks [24], components [32], and method services [12]. Historically, the term fragment was the first one to appear, long before component, chunk, and so on. In this article, we will use the term: "method fragment".

The main role of a method fragment is to provide guidelines to the system engineer for realizing some specific system development activity (for example: specify context of use, user requirement specifications, produce design solutions, evaluate design, etc.) as well as to provide definitions of concepts to be used in this activity [20].

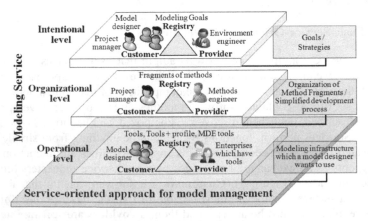

Fig. 4. Three levels of service

In our work, the organizational layer enables the modeling of reusable method fragments. In this layer, the activities are expressed in terms actions on models. The objective is to capitalize method fragments in order to provide them to designers, who have a role in the project group. Customers are, in this case, projects managers which need to define and manage roles and activities in their development process.

The organizational layer uses the operational services in a coordinated way. Project managers can choose some organizational services (part of design process) that require the implementation of operational services for model management. Thus, they create the model management environments for designers involved in their development process.

The **intentional layer** (Figure 4) deals with modeling goals. It conceptualizes strategic modeling needs required by a specialist, a group of specialists, a unity of work or any organization involved in the development process. So, this layer uses the organizational services. The provider corresponds to the environment engineer who plays a new role in charge of the administration and management of the service platform. The customers are still those of the organizational and operational layers, e.g. the models designers and the project managers. For these customers, the services are the goals proposed by the environment engineer (e.g. "Specify an Interactive System").

In this section we introduced the principles of our service-oriented model management approach. In the following sections, we detail the intentional and the organizational levels on the interactive system design methods presented in section 2.

4 Modeling an Intentional Service

This section presents the model of the interactional layer. An **intentional service** is a business-oriented service described from an intentional point of view (e.g. specify an interactive system, study the usability…). It corresponds to the modeling goals. These services are decomposed into elementary services (sub-goals) and so on. Elementary services are specific sub-goals that can be realized by organizational services that correspond to methods fragments (figure 5).

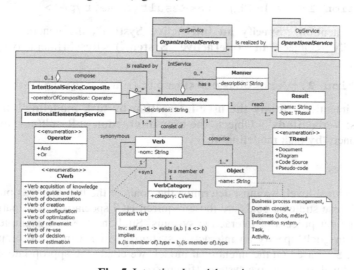

Fig. 5. Intentional model service

The service is characterized by **a verb** that is associated with objects and complemented by a refinement. We have used the ontologies of goals proposes by [11] which describe development's problems. From these ontologies we have identified a set of verbs that describe specific intentions for models management (e.g. **study** interactive system usability, **design** UIs considering users' mental models to perform their task, **automate** the generation of UIs considering many devices ...).

A verb belongs to a **category of verbs**. It corresponds to the type of activities which models designers implement during the development (e.g. the acquisition of knowledge, the guidance and help, documentation ...). In addition, a verb has several **synonymous verbs**. So, synonymous verbs belong to the same category of verbs.

The object is a modeling concept that complements the verb to formulate intentional services (e.g. Interactional Object, Task, Interactive System ...).

The result is an elaborated artifact, modified or used by a service. We take the classification of a result proposed in the unified process [15] and [12]. The types of results identified are: diagrams, documents, source code, and pseudo-codes. **The manner** is a feature that plays specific roles concerning the verb. It corresponds to the way as the service must be realized (e.g. in the purpose to "specify the software architecture with interaction devices choice", the phrase "with interaction devices choice" corresponds to the way to solve the goal achieved.

We use a linguistic approach to formulate an intention. Our purpose is to express the intentional services defined by the meta-model presented in Figure 5. This approach relies on the structural declaration of an intention proposed by Rolland [23]. We have adapted this general statement to the needs of model management. So, in our context work, the structure of an intention is:

Intention: `Verb<Object><Result(name,type)>[Manner]`

The element "Manner" that are in hooks "[]" correspond to optional element. The general structure of the intentions corresponds to several cases. We present below some combinations followed by an example.

Intention 1: `Verb<Object><Result(name,type)>`

For the intention: **"Specify an Interactive System"**, the general structure is: Verb("**Specify**")<Object("**an Interactive System**")><Result(Interactive System, code source>.

Intention 2: `Verb<Object><Result(name,type)>[Manner]`

For the intention: **"Study the user interaction by task modeling"**, the general structure is: Verb("**Study**")<Object("**the user interaction**")>Result(task model, diagram)[Manner("**by task modeling**")].

4.1 Examples

At the intentional level, we must determine the goals of the two methods presented in section 2. These strategic goals are those required HCI specialists, who participate in the development process of interactive systems. Studying the two examples, we define the main goal "specify an interactive system", which can be decomposed into other goals. So, based on the intentional model, we create the appropriate intentional services to develop interactive systems (figure 6).

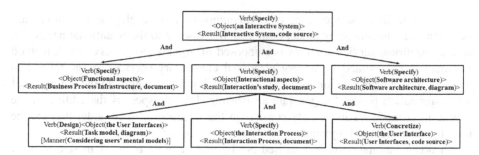

Fig. 6. A composition of intentional services

In the figure above, rectangles correspond to the services and the links describe the composition of intentional services. For example: the service "Specify an Interactive System" is decomposed into three other services: "Specify functional aspects", "Specify interactional aspects" and "Specify software architecture". Similarly, these services can be decomposed. For the sake of conciseness, we concentrate only on the sub-decomposition of the service "Specify Interactional Aspects". It is decomposed intro three other services: "Design the User Interfaces considering users 'mental models", "Specify the Interaction Process" and "Concretize the User Interface". As we will see in the next section, these services are linked to organizational services in order to propose a solution (in terms of processes) to the specified goals.

5 Modeling an Organizational Service

This section presents the model of the organizational layer. Our organizational model service (Figure 7) is inspired by the work of Ralyté et al. [21] who propose a method engineering process model approach, which permits to represent any method as an assembly of the reusable method fragments. In our work, we use the notion of service to support the construction of modeling processes by assembling method fragments.

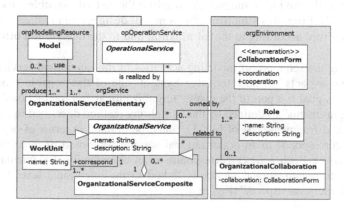

Fig. 7. Organizational model service

An organizational service consists in a composition of development method fragments that can be reused by model designers, in response to the intentional needs. So, an organizational service complex is composed of organizational services. A method fragment is represented by an organizational elementary service that is defined in terms of model manipulation (or actions on models). For example, in the definition of a transformation process to generate an Abstract UI, an aspect is the editing of the source meta-model. This activity consists in the production of a model that can be used by other method fragments.

An organizational service is carried out by one or more roles. A model designer who plays a role can define and reuse several organizational services. At this level, the collaboration term is used for coordination and cooperation tasks between designers [5]. The coordination activities consist of the decomposition of work in activities with similarly goals. The cooperation activities are based on a common modeling goal. Each designer provides their models and the cooperation permits the production of consensual or common models.

The **work unit** defines the action executed during the interactive system design process. It determines in which case the use of organizational service is appropriate (i.e. requirements, analyze, design, validation, implementation,...).

Another aspect considered by our organizational model is the fact that the organizational services are realized by operational services. It means that organizational elementary services must use operational service to support the management of modeling activities.

5.1 Examples

As we have commented in the previous section, we consider that an intentional service can be realized by several organizational services. The criteria for selecting of the objectives are the description of the intentional model. The selection of an appropriate process and a modelling tool is realized from the information contained in the intentional model (for example: the object, the manner and the result). This information will provide a support to simplify the list of possible processes and modelling tools. From this simplification, a model designer can realize the choice of a process or a tool according to the information and to the description offered by the service.

Concerning the sequence of modeling activities of the intentional service "**Specify Interactional aspects**" of an Interactive System, one of the possible processes that answers to this goal is a part of the phase "Organizational and Interactional Specifications of Requirements" as defined by the Symphony method described in section 2.

This method fragment (box of Fig. 1)[2] must be defined in terms of organizational services. It corresponds to an organizational service composed of three sub-services (one by activity). Each activity corresponds to an organizational elementary service. The composite organizational service is linked to the intentional level by the goal: "Specify Interactional aspects" (Figure 8).

---

[2] We do not take into account in this figure the inputs/outputs, or stakeholders. It is only a simplified version of a fragment of the process presented in section 2.

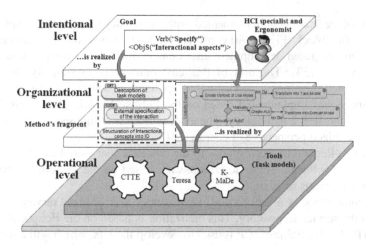

Fig. 8. Relation between an intentional service and an organizational service

The organizational elementary services are described by actions on used or produced models. For example, the activity **"description of task models"** is expressed at the organizational level as an elementary service that carries out the action: "editing of task models". Moreover an organizational service can be supported by several tools defined in terms of operational services. The action "editing of task models" can be carried out by tools with support to task models (CTTE [19], Teresa [3] KMAde [26]...).

Another possible process that answers to the goal **"Specify Interactional aspects"** of an Interactive System is a part of the method engineering for model-driven user interface development proposed by [29]. This goal deals with the UI activities of the role "Usability Expert". They correspond to an organizational service composed of three elementary services: **"Create task model"** to describe task in a hierarchical manner, **"Create context of use model"** to describe the users' characteristics, the platform used and environment; and **"Create domain model"** to describe the manipulated data. As previously, the action "create task model" needs operational services supporting task modeling. These operational services are those (i.e. services for CTTE, Teresa or KMade...) which are already linked to the action "editing of task models".

In this example, we have shown how an intentional service can be realized by two different organizational services. We also illustrate how an organizational service is composed of other organizational services, which can be linked to operational services. To complete this example, we need a support to facilitate the selection of services. In the following sections, we present an overview of the platform that we are currently developing for our service-oriented approach.

6   Platform Support for Service-Oriented Models Management

6.1   Platform Overview

This section presents an experimental prototype which supports our approach. It allows the registration, consultation, research and design of our three services levels.

The prototype has been implemented with two independent but complementary blocks. The first block (Figure 9b) considers the implementation of a service Repository with the integrated development environment for service composition management "ChiSpace" [33]. The aim of this environment is to simplify the work of developers when developing service-based application within domain specific context. ChiSpace was implemented based on the Eclipse Modeling Framework (EMF) platform and the JET 2 technology. The environment is composed of a set of editors within a customized perspective of eclipse [33].

The service Repository corresponds to the database that stored the descriptions of our three services levels. These descriptions are based on the modeling services presented in the previous sections.

The second block is a tool to add, view, select and validate services which are stocked in the service Repository. This realization is based on the Eclipse Rich Client Platform (RCP). So, Eclipse RCP is used to develop the UIs, which will allow use the features of the platform for customers and providers. Figure 9a shows the search intentional services interface. The other UIs are not presented in this article because space constraints. Our prototype currently contains these two blocks. It permits actually, add and search intentional services. We have conceived the UIs for the others services (organizational and operational), but the functionalities of theses UIs are not completed.

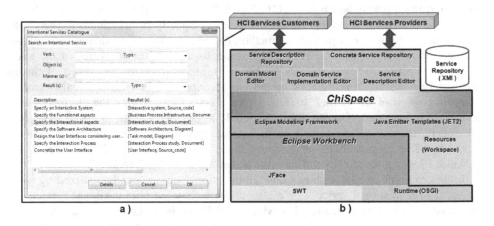

Fig. 9. The service-oriented platform

6.2 Global Vision of Use of the Service-Oriented Platform

Nowadays, we do not have a formal process of helping customers to use the platform. Our global vision is "**top-down** and **bottom-up**". Thus, the platform that we propose can be used in different ways, depending on the needs of customers. Table 1 summarizes some of the scenarios that we have considered.

Table 1. Global vision of use of the service-oriented platform

The vision of Customer. For the customer the goal is search the services depending on their needs.		
	scenario of use	Vision
An intentional support	**From the intention towards the tools**	These examples
	The customer has the intention to study the user interaction and he wants to use a tool which has support to task models without using a modeling process. So, the information concerning to the object, the manner and the result of an intentional service facilitate the request to find the tools required by the user.	correspond to the **top-down** vision in which the modeling environment choice
	From the intention towards the method fragments, then the tools	is a strategic
	The customers must seek and choose an intentional service according to the objectives to reach. The goal selected corresponds at organizational level to organizational services. Then, customers choose among the organizational services associated with the intentional service. Finally, customers can use operational services offering a modeling environment support of the chosen process. This is the process that we illustrate in the previous sections.	decision supported by the selection of modeling goals.
The service dynamic	**From tool towards the method fragments**	The organizational
	The customer knows perfectly one of the tools that he wants to use. However, he needs to rely on processes that suggest using this tool. These processes suggest the use of other tools to complement his work. Par example: a customer knows perfectly KMAde [26] and needs to specify the user interaction for mixed system, then, he explores the organizational services that use this tool. He find that the method proposed by [10] suggest that a complementary tool for the goal of specify the interaction is the tool GuideMe [31].	model service research is guaranteed by a vision **bottom-up**.

7 Conclusion

We have presented in this paper a set of principles of our service-oriented models management approach, designed to helping to model designers in choosing processes and modeling environments adapted to their specific needs. Our work relies on three modeling levels (where providers, customers and services are different): the operational layer to define the modeling environment for model designers; the organizational layer to enable the reuse of operational services in a coordinated way, but also the creation and the management of method fragments; the intentional layer permits to define the modeling goals that can be implemented by design processes described at organizational level.

We also present an overview of the platform under development that will allow the management of our three services levels. Our prototype currently permits add and search intentional services.

Future works include finalizing the service-oriented platform. With the aid of this platform the next step is to test our service-oriented approach in different projects. We consider that our proposal must be able to apply to the other types of services as model transformation, model extraction, etc. It will enable us to validate our propositions and to analyze the impact and the usability of our approach. The evaluation criteria that we will consider are: the facility in the choice of a service, satisfaction of the user related to the services offered by the platform, etc. The realization of user experiments will also enable us to explore other functionalities, and integrated them in our solution. Finally, we plan to propose a formal process of use and operation of the platform to facilitate the modeling activities of model designer.

References

1. Abowd, G., Coutaz, J., Nigay, L.: Structuring the space of interactive system properties. In: Engineering for HCI, vol. A-18, pp. 113–129. North-Holland, Amsterdam (1992)
2. Bastien, J., Scapin, D.-L.: A validation of ergonomic criteria for the evaluation of human-computer interfaces. International Journal of HCI 4, 183–196 (1992)
3. Berti, S., Correani, F., Mori, G., Paternó, F., Santoro, C.: TERESA: A Transformation-Based Environment for Designing Multi-Device Interactive Applications. In: Proc. of CHI 2004, pp. 793–794. ACM Press, New York (2004)
4. Beyer, H., Holtzblatt, K.: Contextual Design. Defining Customer-Systems. Morgan Kaufmann, San Francisco (1998)
5. Blanco, E., Grebici, K., Rieu, D.: A unified framework to manage information maturity in design process. International Journal of Product Development 4(3-4), 255–279 (2007)
6. Brinkkemper, S.: Method Engineering: engineering of information systems development method and tools. Information and Software Technology 38(7) (1996)
7. Calvary, G., Coutaz, J., Thevenin, D., Limbourg, Q., Bouillon, L., Vanderdonckt, J.: A Unifying Reference Framework for Multi-Target User Interfaces. Interacting with Computers 15(3), 289–308 (2003)
8. Constantine, L., Biddle, R., Noble, J.: Usage-centered design and software engineering: Models for integration. In: Proc. of the IFIP TC13 workshop on Closing the gaps: Software engineering and Human-Computer Interaction (2003)
9. Dupuy-Chessa, S., Godet-Bar, G., Pérez-Medina, J.-L., Rieu, D., Juras, D.: Technical and Functional Issues for Integrating Mixed Systems into Information Systems. In: Dubois, E., Gray, P., Nigay, L. (eds.) Engineering of Mixed Reality Systems. Springer, Heidelberg (to appear, 2009)
10. Gauffre, G., Dubois, E., Bastide, R.: Domain-Specific Methods and Tools for the Design of Advanced Interactive Techniques. In: Giese, H. (ed.) MODELS 2008. LNCS, vol. 5002, pp. 65–76. Springer, Heidelberg (2008)
11. Gulliksen, J., Goransson, B.: Usability design: Integrating user-centred systems design in the systems development process. In: Tutorial at CHI 2005, Portland USA (2005)
12. Guzélian, G., Cauvet, C.: SO2M: Towards a Service-Oriented Approach for Method Engineering. In: IKE 2007, Las Vegas USA (2007)
13. Hassine, I., Rieu, D., Bounaas, F., Seghrouchni, O.: Symphony: a conceptual model based on business components. In: SMC 2002, IEEE International Conference on Systems, Man, and Cybernetics, vol. 2 (2002)
14. Hix, D., Hartson, H.: Developing User Interfaces. In: Ensure Usability Through Product & Process., p. 381. John Wiley & Sons, Inc., Chichester (1993)
15. Jacobson, I., Booch, G., Rumbaugh, J.: The Unified Software Development Process. Addison-Wesley, Reading (1999)
16. Kruchten, P.: Introduction of Rational Unified Process, number ISBN 2 212 09104 4. Editions Eyrolles, Paris, France, 282 pages (2000)
17. Papazoglou, M.P.: Service-Oriented Computing: Concepts, Characteristics and Directions. In: 4th International Conference (WISE 2003), pp. 10–12. IEEE CS, Los Alamitos (2003)
18. Papazoglou, M.-P., Traverso, P., Dustdar, S., Leymann, F.: Service-Oriented Computing: A Research Roadmap. In: Dahstuhl Seminar 05462, pp. 1–29 (2005)
19. Paternò, F.: ConcurTaskTrees: An Engineered Notation for Task Models. In: The Handbook of Task Analysis for HCI, pp. 483–503. Lawrence Erlbaum Associates, Mahwah (2003)

20. Ralyté, J., Backlund, P., Kühn, H., Jeusfeld, M.: Method Chunks for Interoperability. In: Embley, D.W., Olivé, A., Ram, S. (eds.) ER 2006. LNCS, vol. 4215, pp. 339–353. Springer, Heidelberg (2006)
21. Ralyté, J., Rolland, C.: An Approach for Method Reengineering. In: Kunii, H.S., Jajodia, S., Sølvberg, A. (eds.) ER 2001. LNCS, vol. 2224, pp. 471–484. Springer, Heidelberg (2001)
22. Redish, J., Wixon, D.: Task analysis: The human-computer interaction, fundamentals, envolving technologies and emerging applications, New York, pp. 922–940 (2003)
23. Rolland, C.: Capturing System Intentionality with Maps. In: Conceptual Modeling in Information Systems Engineering, pp. 141–158. Springer, Berlin (2007)
24. Rolland, C., Plihon, V., Ralyté, J.: Specifying the reuse context of scenario method chunks. In: Pernici, B., Thanos, C. (eds.) CAiSE 1998. LNCS, vol. 1413, p. 191. Springer, Heidelberg (1998)
25. Rosson, M.-B., Carroll, J.-M.: Usability Engineering: Scenario-based Development of Human-Computer Interaction. Academic Press, London (2002)
26. Scapin, D.-L., Lai-Chong Law, E.: Report and Refine Usability Evaluation Methods (R3UEMs). In: COST294-MAUSE 3rd International Workshop, Athens (2007)
27. Shneiderman, B.: Designing the User Interface, 638 p. Addison-Wesley, Reading (1998)
28. Sousa, K., Furtado, E.: From usability tasks to usable user interfaces. In: TAMODIA 2005, pp. 103–110. ACM Press, New York (2005)
29. Sousa, K., Mendonça, H., Vanderdonckt, J.: Towards Method Engineering of Model-Driven User Interface Development. In: Winckler, M., Johnson, H., Palanque, P. (eds.) TAMODIA 2007. LNCS, vol. 4849, pp. 112–125. Springer, Heidelberg (2007)
30. Tarby, J.-C., Barthet, M.-F.: The DIANE+ Method. In: CADUI 1996, Namur, pp. 95–120 (1996)
31. Viala, J., Dubois, E., Gray, P.: GUIDE-ME: graphical user interface for the design of mixed interactive environment based on the ASUR notation. In: UbiMob 2004, Nice France, vol. 64, pp. 74–77 (2004)
32. Wistrand, K., Karlsson, F.: Method components – rationale revealed. In: Persson, A., Stirna, J. (eds.) CAiSE 2004. LNCS, vol. 3084, pp. 189–201. Springer, Heidelberg (2004)
33. Yu, J., Lalanda, P., Chollet, S.: Development Tool for Service-Oriented Applications in Smart Homes. In: Proc. of SCC 2008, DC, USA, pp. 239–246 (2008)

Facilitating Adaptation in Virtual Environments Using a Context-Aware Model-Based Design Process

Johanna Renny Octavia, Lode Vanacken, Chris Raymaekers,
Karin Coninx, and Eddy Flerackers

Hasselt University - tUL - IBBT
Expertise Centre for Digital Media
Wetenschapspark 2, 3590 Diepenbeek, Belgium
{johanna.octavia,lode.vanacken,chris.raymaekers,
karin.coninx,eddy.flerackers}@uhasselt.be

Abstract. Designers and developers of virtual environments have to consider that providing adaptation in virtual environments is important to comply with users' different characteristics. Due to the many possibilities of adaptation that a designer can think of, it is necessary to support the integration of adaptation in the application in a rapid and practical way. We propose to achieve this by adopting the VR-DeMo model-based user interface design (MBUID) process which supports context. In this paper, we strive to integrate adaptation in virtual environments using a context-aware design process and present a validation of this approach with two case studies, namely supporting the adaptation of switching between interaction techniques and adapting the interaction technique itself. These case studies learned us that adaptation can be easily realized using our context-aware model-based design process.

Keywords: Adaptation, virtual environments, context-aware, model-based user interface design.

1   Introduction

Working in virtual environments brings along complex interaction for its users. One difficulty may develop from the vast range of possible 3D interaction techniques employed in virtual environments. This may be cumbersome because the user can not recognize the interaction technique immediately [1]. Users may encounter extraneous cognitive load when having to determine which interaction technique is best for them to use in a certain environment condition. Providing adaptation in virtual environments can be seen as a prospective solution for overcoming this particular problem. Depending on the context of use, the user interface can be adapted for a specific user, based on the user's characteristic [2]. For example, by offering the user only a limited number of interaction techniques derived from the information of his/her preference and ability.

D. England et al. (Eds.): TAMODIA 2009, LNCS 5963, pp. 58–71, 2010.
© Springer-Verlag Berlin Heidelberg 2010

It is our intention to simplify user interaction and make it more natural and intuitive by integrating adaptation into 3D user interfaces in virtual environments. However, the scope of adaptation can be very broad in the sense that there can be many kinds of adaptation to be implemented. Ideally, we would like to support as many adaptations as reasonable from the usability perspective. On the other hand, the integration of such an adaptation in the application may require a lot of ad hoc programming and can bring designers and developers into a lengthy, time-consuming iterative design process. Therefore, we adopt a model-based user interface design (MBUID) process to enable quick prototyping (i.e. by easily modifying diagrams) to investigate the possibility of adaptation in virtual environments. Model-based design approaches have been regularly used to realize implementation of adaptive user interfaces for a broader range of applications over the years, including visual adaptation of user interfaces [3], adaptation for plasticity [4] and website adaptation [5].

In our MBUID approach, we consider adaptation as a form of context. We define context as an artefact influenced by different factors such as user, environment, platform and others. In virtual environments, context can be defined by the internal parameters (e.g. virtual world) and external parameters (e.g. user's characteristics) applied in a certain situation. As we wish to modify those parameters for the purpose of adaptation, we can look at the virtual environment as a context-aware system. Customarily, designing context-aware systems results in low-level programming code that is difficult to maintain. Using MBUID process that supports context, designers and developers are enabled to create context-aware systems in a higher and more abstract level.

In this paper, we describe an approach to integrate adaptation in virtual environments using a context-aware design process. We use the VR-DeMo model-based process [6] in the approach, together with the CoGenIVE tool [7] to support designers and developers in applying our MBUID approach. Further, we will discuss different kinds of adaptation that we want to provide and how our system can be used to support adaptation. The validation of the proposed approach by means of two practical case studies is also discussed in this paper.

2   Adaptation in Virtual Environments

We recognize the significance of supporting adaptation to enhance user interaction in virtual environments. However, we also notice that adaptation in virtual environments is explored less often than in WIMP applications probably partly due to the fact that interaction in virtual environments is more complex. Yet, adaptivity of interaction in virtual environments has been investigated through learning user behavior [8] and user's preferred method of interaction [9].

It is essential that the adaptation should occur according to the current context such as the environment condition of the virtual world and the preferences and abilities of the users. As mentioned earlier, there are many possible forms of adaptation that can be implemented in virtual environments. In this work, we classify adaptation into three types: (I) switching between interaction techniques, (II) adapting the interaction technique itself, and (III) enhancing the interaction technique with modalities. Through our case studies, we would like to investigate the first two types of adaptation as we already experimented with the third type of adaptation in our previous work [10,11].

The first type of adaptation, switching between interaction techniques, involves the action of offering the most suited interaction technique for a user in a certain situation (e.g. environment condition of the virtual world, position of the user). When performing one task in virtual environments, users have the opportunity to choose from several possible interaction techniques to execute the particular task. For example when executing a selection task [1], users may choose between a technique using a virtual hand metaphor and a technique using a virtual pointer metaphor. The choice of interaction techniques can also vary depending on the environment condition or view of the virtual world. In particular, users may prefer one technique over the other when selecting an object in a dense environment, which might be different when in a sparse environment. So, we are interested to investigate the possibility of enabling users to switch between different techniques while performing the same task, as a result of adapting to different environment conditions. We will discuss this in the first case study.

The second type, adapting the interaction technique itself, is basically adjusting the parameters of the interaction technique, which could influence how it should be performed (e.g. motion sensitivity, personal preference). Users have different levels of physical abilities that may affect them when performing an interaction technique in virtual environments. For instance, a user may have a lot of tremor in his hand that decreases his efficiency in accomplishing a selection technique and lessen the accuracy of object selection. To resolve this, we could change certain parameters (e.g. viscosity, force strength) of a task as an adaptation to the user's specific attributes (e.g. degree of tremor). Therefore, we are also intrigued to examine the opportunity of adapting the interaction technique itself by adjusting its sensitivity according to the user's need. This will be the focus of our second case study.

Prior to determining how the adaptation should behave, the designer should assess what the exact need of adaptation is. This includes constructing a user model at design time and acquiring information about the user itself from that model at runtime. A user model plays an important role as a base in the adaptation process of user interfaces to comply with different needs of users. It contains significant information and knowledge about a user's characteristics, which is learned from his traces of interaction with a system/an interface [2]. User characteristics are generally modeled as part of the context description [12]. By closely collaborating with the user model, the adaptation engine will designate the suitable adaptation for a particular user in a particular context.

We are aware of the vital contribution of a user model in providing adaptation in virtual environments. Our previous work [13] constructed a general user model for a target acquisition task in virtual environments. This user model is intended for first-time users, who have no interaction history whatsoever, to benefit straightaway from adaptation in virtual environments. We believe that the idea of supporting adaptation in virtual environments may be realized with the help of context-aware systems.

3   Designing Context-Aware Virtual Environments

In previous work, we presented an approach to design context-aware multimodal virtual environments using the VR-DeMo model-based user interface design process based on an 'Event-Condition-Action' paradigm [11]. The context system made it possible to switch between different modalities for a certain interaction technique based on the context. In this section we shortly introduce this approach and discuss how it can be used for other types of adaptation as well.

The main difference, compared to traditional context-aware systems [14,15], is that the context system resides at the dialog level. More in particular, it is realized using our interaction description model NiMMiT. The graphical notation NiMMiT, inherits the formalism of a state-chart in order to describe the (multimodal) interaction within the virtual environment. Furthermore, it also supports data flow which occurs during the interaction, as well. A more detailed description of NiMMiT can be found in [16].

To support context-dependency in model-based development, three components were realized: context detection, context switching and context handling. Context detection is the process for detecting changes in context, while context switching brings the system in the new state that needs to be supported. Finally, context handling adapts the interaction possibilities to the current context.

With regard to adaptation, the context detection part provides the link with the user model, it will query the user model for information about the conditions which it is checking. The context switching part mostly takes care of actions which should be performed such that the adaptation can occur correctly or that it changes parameters which will adapt the interaction techniques. Finally, the context handling part makes sure that the adaptation can be realized.

In the next sections we will shortly describe the three different parts and an extension on the approach which enables us to also support different context-aware interaction techniques at the dialog level. The case studies elaborate on the practical use of the context system.

3.1   Context Detection and Switching

The realization of the context detection and switching part is performed by adopting 'Event-Condition-Action' rules [17,18]. A certain *event* or combination of events can signal a context switch. After the event has been recognized, certain *conditions* have to be met before switching the context. When these conditions are fulfilled, it might be necessary to first perform some *actions* before finalizing the context switch. For instance, a user may stand up from the chair (*event*). Before executing a context switch, we must ensure that the user wears the tracked gloves (*condition*). If this condition is met, we disable the toolbars needed in a desktop setup and connect the cursor to make the glove visible (*action*).

The context detection and switching will be performed using NiMMiT. Usually, one diagram will be used for detection, listening to the events and checking the conditions, and one for switching, performing the actions. We use two diagrams so that the solution is as modular as possible. Of course, it is possible to integrate both diagrams into one diagram if either the detection or the switching diagram is very simple.

3.2   Context Handling

The context handling part finalizes the context system. The context system needs to be able to create context-aware NiMMiT diagrams that represent the interaction techniques. In this section, we will shortly give an overview of the approach using an example containing context-aware modality selection [10].

In Figure 1, an example of this approach is depicted. Figure 1a shows that in the 'Start'-state several different events (modalities) could trigger the execution of the task chains. Using context information, it is possible to attach a context to a certain event or modality in such a way that depending on the context only the corresponding events are active. If for example 'GLOVE.MOVE' is intended

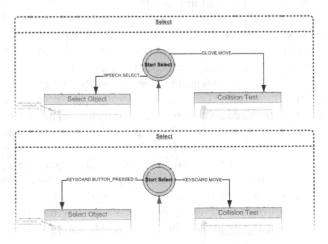

(a) Two NiMMiT diagrams with the same states and event flow, but different events depending on the context

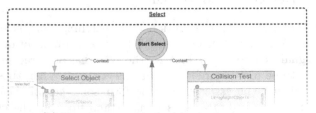

(b) Events were attached to context arrows

Fig. 1. Context Handling [10]

to be used in the immersive setup, one can attach the 'immersive'-context to the event-arrow 'GLOVE.MOVE'. Similarly, the event 'KEYBOARD.MOVE' can be used in the 'desktop'-context.

It is important to note that if there was no support to couple events to a context then the same diagram should be created twice with different events (as in Figure 1a) which obviously would make maintenance much harder. Adding this contextual knowledge to NiMMiT transforms the view of the diagram according to the context. A part of the resulting diagram containing context arrows is shown in Figure 1b.

The approach presented has only been used to switch between modalities at the dialog level. No support for switching between different interaction techniques has been discussed yet. In the next section, we will present an approach to perform context-aware interaction technique selection at the dialog level. It is important to perform this to enable switching between interaction techniques.

3.3   Context-Aware Interaction Technique Selection at the Dialog Level

In Section 2, we introduced three different types of adaptation. The third type (enhancing the interaction technique with modalities) has been realized and investigated in prior work [10,11] and the second type (adapting the interaction technique itself) can be realized in the switching part of the context system without any influence on the model-based design process. To support the first type (switching between interaction techniques), traditionally the task level would be used because of the fact that an interaction technique is similar to a task.

To show the approach which enables designers to switch between interaction techniques using context information, we will use the first case study to explain how the above context system can be used and how it differs from the traditional approaches.

Certain selection techniques are sometimes better suited for a certain context. To exploit this, it should be possible to switch between different interaction techniques. In Figure 2, a task model is presented in which the selection technique can be changed depending on the context. Transforming this task model to the corresponding dialog model will give a similar model as in Figure 3a. When more alternatives would be present, state explosion could occur [14]. To avoid this, we use a combination of our dialog model and NiMMiT.

In the previous section, explaining the context handling, we used NiMMiT and context arrows to be able to differ between modalities depending on the context (see Figure 1). The same approach can also be used to select between tasks depending on the context. To avoid the extra dialog model in Figure 3a, we create a NiMMiT diagram representing the 'Selection' decision task, which then will be used in our dialog model. Merging the both context possibilities into one NiMMiT diagram allows us to merge the two dialog models. This 'Selection'NiMMiT diagram will use context arrows from Section 3.2 to enable to correct interaction technique depending on the context.

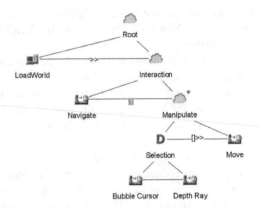

Fig. 2. Task model in which different selection interaction techniques (bubble cursor and depth ray) can be chosen depending on the context

The above approach, applied to the task model from Figure 2 can be seen in Figure 3. Instead of having two dialog models (Figure 3a), one is used containing the 'Selection' decision task (Figure 3b). This 'Selection'-task is represented through a NiMMiT diagram with 'IDLE'-event arrows to the possible interaction techniques (Figure 3c). In order to switch to the correct decision depending on the context, these 'IDLE'-event arrows are assigned to the bubble cursor or depth ray context (Figure 3d).

This strategy might be less intuitive to be performed by a designer. But if the designer is aware of this possibility, it is actually an easy way to support the first type of adaptation, switching between different interaction techniques depending on the context.

4   Case Studies

In this section we introduce two case studies which respectively show how the first and second type (see Section 2) of adaptation are realized using our context system. The same setup is used for both case studies as shown in Figure 4. The input device is a haptic device (Phantom premium) and a stereo screen.

4.1   Adaptation Type I: Switching between Interaction Techniques

Selection experiments [19,20] showed that several aspects of the virtual world influence the performance of selection techniques differently. This means that there is no one best technique in all situations. This information can be used to indicate preferences and provide users with the 'best' selection technique at a right time. However, it should not be surprising that almost all users will slightly deviate from the expected performance for a certain selection technique in a certain environment condition. Because of this, adaptation seems to be a

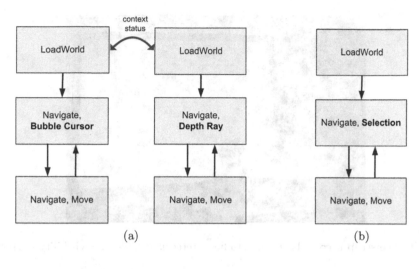

(a)   (b)

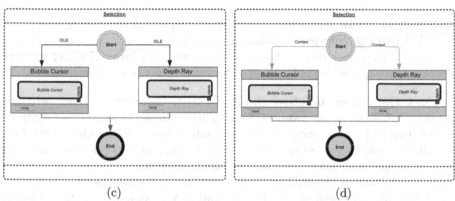

(c)   (d)

Fig. 3. (a) Two dialog models generated from the task model (b) The merged dialog model, containing the 'Selection' decision task (c) NiMMiT Diagram without context arrows, representing the 'Selection' decision task (d) NiMMiT Diagram with context arrows, assigned to the corresponding context (bubble cursor or depth ray), representing the 'Selection' decision task

viable solution to explore. Although in general for all users we know the best technique for a certain situation, a particular user may perform better with another selection technique than the one proposed.

In this case study, we will offer the users two selection techniques based on different metaphors, the 3D bubble cursor (virtual hand) and the depth ray (virtual pointer). Not only because these techniques were found to perform better than the others in dense and occluded virtual environments [20], but also since we have constructed a user model [13] based on our selection experiment in different environment density conditions (sparse versus dense) and occlusion conditions (visible versus occluded). We will use the user model in combination with the

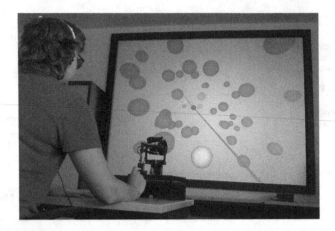

Fig. 4. The setup used in both case studies (stereo is disabled for visibility purposes)

current viewpoint of the user on the virtual world. Based on this viewpoint, we will derive the current environment condition (e.g. very sparse scene and almost no objects occluding each other). Then, we will provide the user with the selection technique which is best suited for him in this particular condition.

Context Detection and Switching. Usually, the detection and switching diagram are split to have a more modular solution. However in this case study, no actions need to be performed after a new context has been detected. Therefore, we will combine the detection and switching diagram into one diagram since there is no reason to have a separate switching diagram.

First an initialization step ('Start'-state to the 'Init'-task chain) is performed (see Figure 5). This step queries for the initial context and executes an initial switch to that context ('FireContextEvent'). This task makes the system fire a context event, which is usually used by the switching diagram to know which actions should be performed. We keep on firing the event because it could be used by other diagrams too. Since the switching diagram finalizes the context switch, we immediately perform the 'SetContext'-task. Due to the fact that the different contexts (i.e. different selection techniques) are chosen by evaluating the same conditions in the 'CheckViewpoint'-task, we only use one state instead of one state per context situation as we showed in previous work [11].

We want to provide the user with different selection techniques depending on the viewpoint. Therefore the 'CAMERA.MOVE'-event, the event fired when the viewpoint changes, indicates a possible context switch (*event*). When this event occurs, the viewpoint will be checked for the current environment condition. We will check for the amount of objects in the current viewpoint to assess the density of the objects. In combination with the density, we will also calculate how many objects overlap with each other so we can estimate the possibility that a user wants to select an occluded target (*condition*). By knowing the current environment condition, we can simply utilize the user model of the particular user

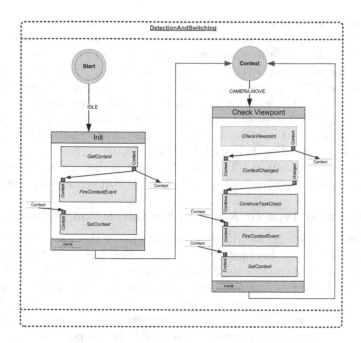

Fig. 5. Context detection and switching diagram - Case Study 1

to decide which selection technique should be chosen. The user model provides information about the most suitable selection technique for a user linked to a particular environment condition based on the user's performance and preference (e.g. the bubble cursor technique in the dense and occluded condition).

When the 'CAMERA.MOVE'-event occurs and the viewpoint is checked ('CheckViewpoint'), we calculate the current context. To assure we only fire context change events when the context has changed, we add a construction that checks if the context has changed ('ContextChanged'). If the context has changed, we output 'true' and then the context switches, else we output 'false'. The 'ContextChanged'-task can be seen as an extra condition to check before a new context is detected. The task that is responsible for checking the condition must collect its result in a boolean label. This label is passed on to a predefined task 'ContinueTaskChain', which checks whether or not the condition is fulfilled. When the boolean contains the value 'true', nothing happens and then the task chain is continued. When the value is 'false', this task throws an exception and activates the exception handling mechanism of the NiMMiT task chain. The current task chain is interrupted and the previous state is restored. This means that when the condition is not met, the original state is restored and no context switching event is generated.

Context Handling. The handling part has to enable the correct selection technique depending on the context. We use the approach described in Section 3.3. The NiMMiT diagram presented in Figure 3d is the diagram which we will use in this case study, depending on the current context, the correct 'IDLE'-event arrow will be active so the correct selection technique will be activated.

There might be an issue when the context changes but a certain selection technique is already active. In the solution presented here, the selection technique currently active will not be aborted and the other selection technique can only become active after the selection is performed. While some applications might prefer this behaviour, it should also be possible to abort the current selection technique and enable the other selection technique. To realize this, an action would need to be added to change a label that tells the current running selection technique to stop immediately. The main drawback is that we need to change the selection technique itself by incorporating this aborting-check using the label.

4.2   Adaptation Type II: Adapting the Interaction Technique Itself

In the second case study, we will show an example of the second type of adaptation where we change parameters of an interaction technique to influence the performance of the technique itself. In particular, we want to detect if a user's hand exhibits tremor during interaction and make such an adaptation to help reducing the hand motion tremor. For this purpose, we will use force feedback to enable applying viscosity to the input device which in the end will reduce the tremor. If no haptic device is available, it could also be possible to reduce the tremor using a low-pass filtering approach. A viscosity force is calculated using the velocity and a constant defined by the designer, where a high amount of viscosity feels like moving your hand in water.

We introduce three discrete levels of tremor (low, medium and high). In case of a low amount of tremor, we do not apply any viscosity because it is normal that the user's hand has some tremor during movement. For a medium and high amount of tremor, we apply two different constants that are defined manually.

Context Detection and Switching. This case study will use two separate diagrams for detection and switching. The context detection diagram is very similar to the one of the previous case study (see Figure 5). However, there are two differences between the diagrams in both case studies. The first difference is the replacement of the 'CheckViewpoint'-task by a 'CheckTremor'-task, which tries to calculate the tremor of the hand. Calculating hand tremor is rather difficult and different mechanisms can be used depending on the target population [21]. We have implemented a straightforward approach, we use the velocity of the user's hand as an indication for the degree of tremor. We buffer the velocity for a few seconds and check how many times its magnitude changes from speeding up or slowing down and vice versa.

The second difference is the removal of the 'SetContext'-task from the context detection diagram, which is now inside the switching diagram. The switching diagram, represented in Figure 6, is fairly simple. It listens to the context events fired by the detection diagram and sets the corresponding viscosity constant depending on the degree of tremor.

This case study provides three different discrete levels of adaptation with regard to the tremor ('LOW', 'MEDIUM' and 'HIGH' degree of tremor). This

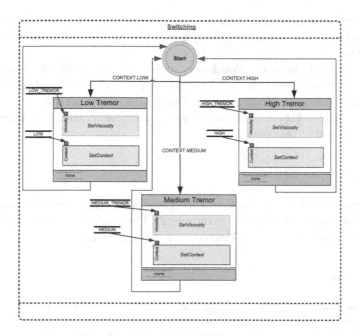

Fig. 6. Context switching diagram - Case Study 2

solution might not be flexible enough, some designers may want to use a continuous scale instead. Note that other parameters might also have either a discrete or a continuous scale. It is possible to use continuous levels in the second case study. Instead of using three context levels, we would use two levels which indicate either 'LOWER' or 'HIGHER' degree of tremor. If we keep on detecting tremor, we could keep on firing the 'HIGHER' context as being detected[1] and keep on raising the viscosity constant. Otherwise if the tremor decreases, we can fire the 'LOWER' context as being detected (using the 'FireContextEvent'-task).

Context Handling. This adaptation only changes certain parameters of interaction techniques. It does not require another task chain to be executed depending on the context (adaptation type I) or other modalities to be enabled/disabled (adaptation type III). Therefore, the context handling part is not necessary to be applied in the system for realizing the second type of adaptation.

5 Conclusion

In this paper we showed how VR-DeMo, a context-aware model-based design process for virtual environments, can be used to support designers and developers to facilitate rapid development and prototyping of adaptation in virtual environments. We identified three possible types of adaptation and validated

---

[1] The 'ContextChanged'-task has to be removed from the detection diagram.

the proposed approach using case studies. These case studies showed that our context-aware model-based process is feasible to explore adaptation in virtual environments.

For future work, from the developers' point of view, it might be interesting to further investigate how the user model could be more easily integrated in the context detection part of the system. From a usability perspective, we would like to further investigate how users react on adaptation that is realized by the system presented in this paper.

Acknowledgments

Part of the research at EDM is funded by the ERDF (European Regional Development Fund) and the Flemish government. The work described in this paper is funded by the transnational University Limburg (tUL).

References

1. Bowman, D.A., Kruijff, E., LaViola, J.J., Poupyrev, I.: 3D User Interfaces, Theory and Practice. Addison-Wesley, Reading (2005)
2. Rich, E.: Users are individuals: individualizing user models. International Journal Human-Computer Studies 51, 323–338 (1999)
3. Nilsson, E.G., Floch, J., Hallsteinsen, S., Stav, E.: Model-based user interface adaptation. In: Davies, N., Kirste, T., Schumann, H. (eds.) Mobile Computing and Ambient Intelligence: The Challenge of Multimedia, Internationales Begegnungs- und Forschungszentrum fuer Informatik (IBFI), Schloss Dagstuhl, Germany (2005)
4. Sottet, J.S., Ganneau, V., Calvary, G., Coutaz, J., Favre, J.M., Demumieux, R.: Model-driven adaptation for plastic user interfaces. In: Baranauskas, C., Palanque, P., Abascal, J., Barbosa, S.D.J. (eds.) INTERACT 2007. LNCS, vol. 4662, pp. 397–410. Springer, Heidelberg (2007)
5. Ceri, S., Dolog, P., Matera, M., Nejdl, W.: Model-driven design of web applications with client-side adaptation. In: Koch, N., Fraternali, P., Wirsing, M. (eds.) ICWE 2004. LNCS, vol. 3140, pp. 201–214. Springer, Heidelberg (2004)
6. Coninx, K., De Troyer, O., Raymaekers, C., Kleinermann, F.: VR-DeMo: a tool-supported approach facilitating flexible development of virtual environments using conceptual modelling. In: Virtual Concept 2006, Cancun, Mexico (2006)
7. De Boeck, J., Raymaekers, C., Coninx, K.: A tool supporting model based user interface design in 3d virtual environments. In: GRAPP 2008, Funchal, Portugal (2008)
8. Celentano, A., Nodari, M., Pittarello, F.: Adaptive interaction in web3d virtual worlds. In: Proceedings of the 9th 3D Web, pp. 41–50 (2004)
9. Wingrave, C.A., Bowman, D.A., Ramakrishnan, N.: Towards preferences in virtual environment interfaces. In: Proceedings of the 8th EGVE, pp. 63–72 (2002)
10. Vanacken, L., Cuppens, E., Clerckx, T., Coninx, K.: Extending a dialog model with contextual knowledge. In: Winckler, M., Johnson, H., Palanque, P. (eds.) TAMODIA 2007. LNCS, vol. 4849, pp. 28–41. Springer, Heidelberg (2007)
11. Vanacken, L., De Boeck, J., Raymaekers, C., Coninx, K.: Designing context-aware multimodal virtual environments. In: IMCI 2008, Chania, Crete, Greece, pp. 129–136 (2008)

12. Preuveneers, D., Van den Bergh, J., Wagelaar, D., Georges, A., Rigole, P., Clerckx, T., Berbers, Y., Coninx, K., Jonckers, V., Bosschere, K.D.: Towards an Extensible Context Ontology for Ambient Intelligence. In: Markopoulos, P., Eggen, B., Aarts, E., Crowley, J.L. (eds.) EUSAI 2004. LNCS, vol. 3295, pp. 148–159. Springer, Heidelberg (2004)
13. Octavia, J.R., Raymaekers, C., Coninx, K.: Investigating the possibility of adaptation and personalization in virtual environments. In: Houben, G., McCalla, G., Pianesi, F., Zancanaro, M. (eds.) UMAP 2009. LNCS, vol. 5535, pp. 361–366. Springer, Heidelberg (2009)
14. Clerckx, T.: Model-Based Development of Context-Aware Interactive Applications in Ambient Intelligence Environments. PhD thesis, transnationale Universiteit Limburg (2007)
15. Pribeanu, C., Limbourg, Q., Vanderdonckt, J.: Task modelling for context-sensitive user interfaces. In: Johnson, C. (ed.) DSV-IS 2001. LNCS, vol. 2220, pp. 49–68. Springer, Heidelberg (2001)
16. De Boeck, J., Vanacken, D., Raymaekers, C., Coninx, K.: High-level modeling of multimodal interaction techniques using nimmit. Journal of Virtual Reality and Broadcasting 4 (2007)
17. Beer, W., Christian, V., Ferscha, A., Mehrmann, L.: Modeling Context-aware Behavior by Interpreted ECA Rules. In: Kosch, H., Böszörményi, L., Hellwagner, H. (eds.) Euro-Par 2003. LNCS, vol. 2790, pp. 1064–1073. Springer, Heidelberg (2003)
18. Etter, R., Costa, P., Broens, T.: A Rule-Based Approach Towards Context-Aware User Notification Services. In: ICPS 2006, pp. 281–284 (2006)
19. Poupyrev, I., Weghorst, S., Billunghurst, M., Ichikawa, T.: Egocentric object manipulation in virtual environments; empirical evalutaion of interaction techniques. Computer Graphics Forum 17, 30–41 (1998)
20. Vanacken, L., Grossman, T., Coninx, K.: Multimodal selection techniques for dense and occluded 3d virtual environments. International Journal on Human Computer Studies 67, 237–255 (2009)
21. Duval, C., Sadikot, A., Panisset, M.: The detection of tremor during slow alternating movements performed by patients with early Parkinson's disease. Experimental Brain Research 154, 395–398 (2004)

Task Models for Safe Software Evolution and Adaptation

Jan Van den Bergh, Deepak Sahni, and Karin Coninx

Hasselt University - tUL - IBBT
Expertise Centre for Digital Media
Wetenschapspark 2, 3590 Diepenbeek, Belgium
firstname.lastname@uhasselt.be

Abstract. Many industrial applications have large and complex interfaces that grow incrementally over time. Typically, these interfaces will be used by people with different user profiles. The combination of these facts demands a software methodology and tool support that ideally allow consistency checks and configuration in order to avoid a system to become unusable. In this paper, we present an approach in which task models are used throughout the design and development cycle up to the final application. The task model is not only used at design time, but is also used to check for potential problems with e.g. consistency during configuration of the final application.

Keywords: Customization, task model, evolution, consistency, model-based user interface design.

1 Introduction

The task model has been one of the central models in several model-based and model-driven development approaches [1,2,3]. This central role has been based on the fact that it offers a structured overview of the tasks that have to be performed by a user. Furthermore, a notation such as ConcurTaskTrees also allows for checking properties such as reachability, reversibility and mutual awareness [4] although the currently tools do not have support for these capabilities.

When considering approaches for large industrial applications, adoption of a model-based development cycle meets some resistance even while offering these benefits. This is especially the case when the application is not safety critical, but can still be mission critical. This resistance has multiple reasons. For instance, many methodologies [1,2,5], require other abstract models, such as the abstract user interface model, besides the task model. This makes it more difficult to integrate the approach in current development practices. Not only is it difficult to integrate the approach in current design and development practices, it also requires the development team to learn a set of new languages or notations.

In this paper, we propose a methodology that takes the "one model, many interfaces" phrase introduced by Paternò [6] to the extreme. The methodology uses only one abstract model, the ConcurTaskTrees model, and integrates with

D. England et al. (Eds.): TAMODIA 2009, LNCS 5963, pp. 72–77, 2010.

user-centered software engineering practices. This model is not only used during analysis and design phases, but also during prototyping and even after product development to generate the navigation structure of the application's user interface. Another innovative use is that the temporal operators are also used during customization to avoid logical errors in the execution due to the removal of (seemingly) irrelevant tasks.

2   A One-Model User-Centered Process

We will use the MuiCSer process framework [7] as a basis for discussing how we envision the usage of the task model at different stages in a user-centered design and development process that supports user interface evolution. The different phases of the MuiCSer process instantiation are shown at the right side of Fig. 1, while the usage of the task model is shown in the form of notes at the left-hand side.

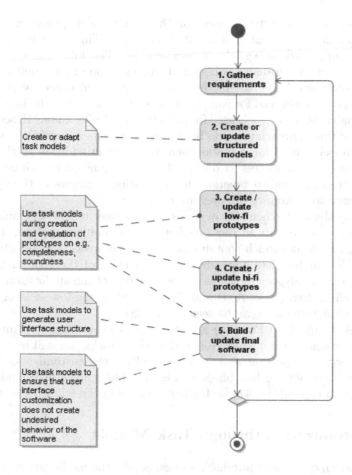

Fig. 1. A MuiCSer process instantiation and the envisioned use of the task model

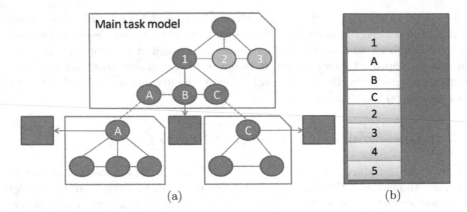

Fig. 2. (a) Task model distribution over files (pentagons) and links with software components (boxes) and, (b) the corresponding navigation structure

The task model is actively used for the first time in phase two, in which structured models are created or updated (analysis). This phase in the proposed process is supported by e.g. the Teresa tool [3]. The following two phases in the MuiCSer process framework deal with the creation of low-fidelity and high-fidelity prototypes. Using the methodology proposed in earlier work [8], these prototypes can be checked for completeness and soundness with the task model using a small tool. Many tools used for prototyping [7] offer the XML serialization required for this approach to work. In the fifth phase mentioned shown in Fig. 1, the task model is used for two additional purposes in addition to checking for completeness and soundness as during the prototyping phases three and four. The task model is used to generate the navigation structure of the application and it is used to customize the user interface.

Fig. 2(a) shows a schematic overview of the task model and links it with the software components in our proof-of-concept implementation. There is a main task model file, which contains at least three layers, and possibly several separate files further detailing subtasks. Each child of the root task (1, 2, 3, ...) represents a category in the navigation system of the application, while the root's grandchildren (tasks A, B and C) are used as the lowest level entries of the navigation system, as can be seen in Fig. 2(b).

Tasks A, B and C in Fig. 2(a) are connected to the software components of which the system is comprised. Notice that these tasks can still have subtasks. This property is important as it will be used for the customization of the final product (during the last phase in Fig. 1). The role of task models in the customization capabilities will be further detailed in the following section.

3   Customization through Task Models

Customization of the user interface, and especially the modification of the tasks that are available in a specific deployment of the application, is an important issue in complex industrial applications. The needs of the companies deploying these applications greatly differs and even within one company the needs can greatly differ depending on the person that is using the application.

As described in the previous section, the task model is the piece of information that links all different components of the user interface. If is therefore a logical choice to also use it to enable customization of the user interface and more specifically to remove or to disable parts of the user interface.

The hierarchical structure and temporal relations of a task model such as ConcurTaskTrees describe dependencies between task. One example of such a dependency occurs when information is exchanged between different tasks [9]. When such dependencies are present, it has of course a great impact on the capability to remove tasks (and thus parts of the user interface) from the system.

Table 1 shows the effect of removing one task on the other tasks in the task model for the different binary temporal operators. We used the following guideline within our customization algorithm: when a task or the correctness of the task model depends on the result, including the successful termination, of another task, the former task will be removed when the latter is removed. Based on this guideline the following factors were determined to cause a dependency between tasks:

information exchange. When information exchange is explicitly modeled in the task model, we assume that the information exchanged by the tasks is crucial for a correct execution of the tasks and therefore they share a mutual dependency.

deactivation. When a task deactivates another task, removing the latter task completely changes the meaning of the task model and may even cause an otherwise correct task model to never end. E.g. when the infinite iteration operator is applied to the deactivated task.

enabling. When the task that precedes an enabling operator is removed, the task following the operator is also removed, because it has to much influence on the meaning of a task model. E.g. removing a login-task could result in unauthorized users having access to some functionality.

4   Discussion

This paper discussed a process that uses a single model throughout development: the task model, which is directly linked to parts of the user interface. This has the advantage that the traceability problem of requirements is minimized, which is considered to be an important property of a development process [10]. The process outlined in this paper has been used as part of a research and development project [8]. During this project the last two phases of the process have been carried out on prototypes instead of on a real system. Proof-of-concept implementations of the proposed tools have been realized and used during the project. This enabled us to do a preliminary evaluation of these tools during which we noticed that there are several enhancements that need to be made before these tools could be used in a real-life setting.

Table 1. Binary temporal operators of ConcurTaskTrees and effect when removing one of the involved tasks in our customization algorithm

Operator		Removed Task	Effect
Name	Notation		
Choice	T1[]T2	T1	T2 stays
		T2	T1 stays
Concurrency	T1 |[]| T2	T1	T2 removed
with information exchange		T2	T1 removed
Independent Concurrency	T1 ||| T2	T1	T2 stays
		T2	T1 stays
Order Independence	T1 | = | T2	T1	T2 stays
		T2	T1 stays
Deactivation	T1 [> T2	T1	T2 stays
		T2	T1 removed
Suspend Resume	T1 | > T2	T1	T2 stays
		T2	T1 stays
Enabling	T1 >> T2	T1	T2 removed
		T2	T1 stays
Enabling	T1 [] >> T2	T1	T2 removed
with information exchange		T2	T1 stays

A first enhancement is better integration between the task model tool and the design tool. A designer should not be forced to modify XML by hand to link the task model to a user interface component. A plugin for the design environment can improve this situation.

A second concern is the customization of the software. Informal tests of the customization feature revealed that there is a definite need for the user to see what the impact will be of selecting/deselecting a task from the task model. Due to the dependency rules discussed in the previous section, removal of a single leaf-task can result in the removal of a significant part of the task model (and thus also the applications features in the user interface). The user should be informed about the consequences of his actions before he takes them. Some aspects of the work on feature models, such as that by Czarnecki et al. [11] may also be useful in realizing the user interface customization using task models.

Another point of future work, besides further validation and refinement of the approach, is to investigate whether the customization feature can be combined with the idea of executable task models proposed Klug and Kangasharju [9].

Finally, during the project mentioned before, we were constantly reminded that there should be more clear advantages of using task models before they will be actively used for large industrial applications. Transparent integration of additional model checking capabilities in task modeling tools could influence the decision to use a task-based approach such as the one proposed in this paper as part of regular industrial development. Further research regarding formalization of task models and related tool support therefore seems warranted. Also a direct relation between the task model and usability properties of the final user interface and automated checking thereof would be highly appreciated.

Acknowledgments

This research was performed in the context of the IWT project Warhol of Punch Graphix in cooperation with researchers of IBBT-CUO (KULeuven). Part of the research at the Expertise Centre for Digital Media is funded by the ERDF (European Regional Development Fund) and the Flemish Government.

References

1. Wolff, A., Forbrig, P.: Deriving user interfaces from task models. In: Proc. of MD-DAUI 2009. Ceur-ws.org, vol. 439 (2009),
   http://ceur--ws.org/Vol--439/paper8.pdf
2. Calvary, G., Coutaz, J., Thevenin, D., Limbourg, Q., Bouillon, L., Vanderdonckt, J.: A Unifying Reference Framework for multi-target user interfaces. Interacting with Computers 15, 289–308 (2003)
3. Mori, G., Paternò, F., Santoro, C.: Design and development of multidevice user interfaces through multiple logical descriptions. IEEE Transactions on Sofware Engineering 30, 507–520 (2004)
4. Paternò, F., Santoro, C.: Integrating model checking and HCI tools to help designers verify user interface properties. In: Palanque, P., Paternó, F. (eds.) DSV-IS 2000. LNCS, vol. 1946, pp. 135–150. Springer, Heidelberg (2001)
5. Sottet, J.S., Ganneau, V., Calvary, G., Coutaz, J., Demeure, A., Favre, J.M., Demumieux, R.: Model-driven adaptation for plastic user interfaces. In: Baranauskas, C., Palanque, P., Abascal, J., Barbosa, S.D.J. (eds.) INTERACT 2007. LNCS, vol. 4662, pp. 397–410. Springer, Heidelberg (2007)
6. Paternò, F., Santoro, C.: One model, many interfaces. In: Kolski, C., Vanderdonckt, J. (eds.) CADUI, pp. 143–154. Kluwer, Dordrecht (2002)
7. Haesen, M., Coninx, K., Van den Bergh, J., Luyten, K.: Muicser: A process framework for multi-disciplinary user-centred software engineering processes. In: Forbrig, P., Paternò, F. (eds.) HCSE/TAMODIA 2008. LNCS, vol. 5247, pp. 150–165. Springer, Heidelberg (2008)
8. Van den Bergh, J., Haesen, M., Luyten, K., Notelaers, S., Coninx, K.: Toward multi-disciplinary model-based (re)design of sustainable user interfaces. In: Graham, T.C.N., Palanque, P. (eds.) DSV-IS 2008. LNCS, vol. 5136, pp. 161–166. Springer, Heidelberg (2008)
9. Klug, T., Kangasharju, J.: Executable task models. In: Proceedings of TAMODIA, pp. 119–122. ACM, New York (2005)
10. Sousa, K., Mendonca, H., Vanderdonckt, J.: User Interface Development Lifecycle for Business-Driven Enterprise Applications. In: Computer-Aided Design of User Interfaces VI, pp. 23–34. Springer, Heidelberg (2009)
11. Czarnecki, K., Helsen, S., Eisenecker, U.W.: Staged configuration through specialization and multilevel configuration of feature models. Software Process: Improvement and Practice 10, 143–169 (2005)

Coherent Task Modeling and Execution Based on Subject-Oriented Representations

Albert Fleischmann[1], Sonia Lippe[2], Nils Meyer[1], and Christian Stary[3]

[1] jCOM1 AG, Lilienthalstraße 17, 85296 Rohrbach, Germany
{albert.fleischmann,nils.meyer}@jcom1.com
[2] SAP Research, 133 Mary Street, Brisbane, QLD 4000, Australia
sonia.lippe@sap.com
[3] JKU, Business Informatics, Freistädterstraße 315, 4040 Linz, Austria
Christian.Stary@jku.at

Abstract. Process- and task-driven workflow support has become vital for enterprises as they operate in an increasingly networked business environment. Thereby business process specifications represent boundary objects not only between different organizational units, but also between technology and business operations. Process specifications need to be integrated and implemented in a flexible way for actual work-task support. Although several business process techniques and technologies are in place there are still several transformational steps to be performed when implementing business operations based on detailed work descriptions. One effective way to prevent incoherencies is role-specific and task-driven modeling, representation, and processing of business operations. The introduced approach is termed subject-oriented business process management, as it ensures coherence between modeling and execution through focusing on the communication flow among process participants (subjects) in the course of work- task accomplishment.

1 Introduction

The competitiveness of enterprises is increasingly determined by their capability to implementing process and task-driven workflow support enabling structural flexibility, besides high quality of products and services, cost effectiveness, and working partner/customer relationships [14]. This need for velocity has been identified when cross-enterprise operations had become relevant in the course of economic globalization. Structural flexibility requires adapting to global supply chains or evolving service networks albeit increasing operational efficiency and effectiveness [5]. Both require focusing on roles and work tasks, such as for accounting (cf. [7]).

When specifying (cross-) organizational operations process models at various levels of detail are tailored to a specific business. Of particular importance is their coherence, in particular, when different organizational roles or organizational units are involved in a business case. *Coherence* requires the consistent propagation of business objectives to operational structures, e.g., reducing service cycle times through reporting loops, both on the level of process specification, *and* on the level of processing them, e.g., using workflow management systems. Work tasks and their execution

D. England et al. (Eds.): TAMODIA 2009, LNCS 5963, pp. 78–91, 2010.
© Springer-Verlag Berlin Heidelberg 2010

can be considered as functional entities with dedicated objectives and particularities that have to be integrated with those of the enterprise network or networked enterprise. They have to be part of intelligible and flexible representational schemes for workflow support to keep up with the required dynamics of change. The (re-) design of work processes has to be tightly coupled to control flows of enterprise information systems (cf. [10]).

In the course of specification targeting towards implementation, a language switch occurs from natural to formal or at least, diagrammatic languages. Effects of that shift are of economical (costs), social (conflicts, negotiations), and organizational scale (iterations, quality control). Those effects are perpetuated when dealing with different types of changes due to the snapshot nature of the modeling process and the resulting representations (cf. [8], p.15). This situation is likely to lead to incoherent transformation of information throughout analysis, design, and implementation of workflow support systems. It has been termed semantic gap, and could not be resolved so far (cf. [3]). It escalates once tasks are increasingly pushed to users [1]. Consequently, our research targets towards semantically correct flow of control on the level of work tasks that allows automatically generating (syntactically correct) workflows on the level of technology support.

In case of automated process execution the control flow is provided by a process definition. It contains information to initiate, monitor, and complete the execution of corresponding actions. Although this concept stems from manufacturing handling production lines, it can be applied to service industries, as business process definitions contain at least a sequence of work steps [2]. In doing so, all business activities are considered in the same way as production lines. The various activities of a process are ordered in a sequence and organized around processing of a production element.

However, there are major differences between traditional production processes and business processes. For production major operations focus on the production object - the workstations involved in the production line do not need to interact intensively. At a production workstation certain production steps are executed. After that the production object is transported to another workstation along the production line where the next production step is performed. Business processes are much more interactive. In service industries, such as banking, the employees involved in a process interact intensively in contrast to employees working along a production line. As a consequence, successful service processes require a high degree of interaction among processes, in particular organizational entities. This fact has to be taken into account when designing and executing (cross-organizational) business processes.

Common modeling languages, such as ARIS [11], hardly allow for the description of business processes in terms of structured interactions between individual participants and/or their role definition in the process. Most of the languages focus on the sequence of activities, e.g., functions in ARIS, and the resulting flow of control. Sticking to this type of flow hinders business transformation and process automation, as emphasized recently for service-oriented architecting of software systems (cf. [15]). In order to overcome this deficiency, subject-oriented languages promote role-specific specification of work tasks and interaction along task accomplishment. Such an approach also reduces semantic gaps when modeling, while ensuring syntactically correct flow of control (cf. [13]).

In the following we introduce this novel paradigm by detailing the concept and comparing it to existing schemes for (cross-) organizational business development. In section 2 we introduce the constituents of subject-oriented modeling, and the basic arrangement (choreography) of its representations. Section 3 addresses the flow of control represented in the subject-oriented models. In section 4 we discuss the JPASS! suite guiding (cross-) organizational developments. Section 5 concludes the paper reflecting our achievements and detailing our future research.

2 Representing Subjects

In this section we motivate the choreography (rather than the orchestration) of process-oriented work models in section 2.1, in particular when striving for executable specifications, before introducing the structure of subject-oriented modeling in section 2.2.

2.1 Designing for Self-control

Model-driven process execution becomes increasingly important in the context of interoperable business operations and the resulting execution of (cross-) organizational work processes. In this context the ultimate goal is to achieve an integrated modeling approach and tool support maintaining the task perspective while constructing executable process models. Lippe et al. have identified three contingent levels for business process modeling and refinement [9]:

- A business level to express the stakeholders needs from a business point of view.
- A technical level which provides a more detailed description in terms of ICT representations
- An execution level where processes are specified in a platform-dependent manner that can be executed by an engine, such as BPEL.

For process execution orchestration and choreography have been proposed (cf. [6]): Choreography describes processes in a collaborative way. For each party involved in the process its part in the interaction and communication between partners handled via messages is described. For orchestration the execution order of steps and interactions within an organization is captured. In this case, each process is always controlled by one of the involved parties.

Considering privacy requirements, stemming in particular from networks involving competing partners, an orchestration-like, central flow of control is not acceptable for the partners. Hence, task execution, especially in low-trust situations, such as evolving business networks, has to follow a choreographed approach. In that case, each partner controls its own processes, and messages are exchanged in the course of collaboration. In order to achieve model-driven execution, models are required that show the processes in a more collaborative way, where each partner involved describes the process from its perspective, including the resulting exchange of messages. Such a procedure is required on all levels of modeling.

Applying the scheme to (cross-) organizational business-process modeling languages as defined by Lippe et al. [9] we could analyze to which extent existing business-process languages meet the demands rising from the described situation.

Table 1. Checking Business Process-Modeling Languages

0 = not supported; 1 = supported; 0.5 = partially supported.

Description	Modeling Language				
	EPC[a]	WS-CDL[b]	BPMN[c]	UML[d]	BPEL[e]
Modeling of overall flow and logical sequence of work steps	1	1	1	1	0
Modeling of participants in process-driven task execution	1	1	0.5	0	1
Modeling of message exchange between participants	0	1	0.5	0	0.5
Modeling of process from perspective of each participant (internally) and its message exchange (externally)	0	0.5	0.5	0.5	0.5
Information hiding of internal task processing	0.5	0.5	0.5	0.5	1

[a] [11], [b] http://www.w3.org/TR/ws-cdl-10/#Notational-Conventions,
[c] http://www.omg.org/spec/BPMN/1.1/pdf, [d] http://www.omg.org, [e] http://www.bpmi.org

The table reveals that integrated support for participant- and communication-oriented modeling is still an open issue. EPCs, BPMN, BPEL, and UML focus on function-based modeling, and allow information about participants as context of functions. Interaction/communication-oriented modeling between participants acting in processes is only partially supported. However, the interaction perspective needs to be addressed on both levels, the technical and business level, in case the mapping of business entities to a technical (information or workflow) components and flow control should not lack coherence. From that dual perspective business processes have to be considered as a set of structured interactions between actors handling a business opportunity or performing a task. Interactions might involve organizations, roles or organizational units of an organization, applications or a combination of those, as shown in the following.

2.2 Subject-Oriented Modeling

Driven by the demand for streamlining specifications when addressing the technical and business level, we have developed a technique where task accomplishment is described from the perspective of the actors involved in a process, and the organizational workflow are captured as intertwined actor-driven task procedures. The approach implements theories provided by Robin Milner and C.A.R. Hoare. It has been implemented in the jPASS! suite based on the PASS concept [4] bringing users in control of task execution. They are in the center of business-process management actions. Users (Subjects) in that context can be persons, software applications or a combination of both, meaning that data is being entered to a software application.

Work-task accomplishment and execution are considered as structured interactions of subjects involved in a business process. Subjects transfer information and coordinate their work by exchanging messages. Messages can be exchanged synchronously, asynchronously or in a combined form. The synchronization type can be specified using a corresponding message type and a sending subject. Each subject has an input pool as a mailbox for incoming messages. The synchronization type is defined by attributes of the input pool.

The following figures show the subjects and messages exchanged along a simple vacation application process. It exemplifies the behavior of a subject Employee. The state ´work´ is the initial state of the subject. Figure 2 reveals the interaction between an employee and the management. Each subject sends and receives messages and accomplishes some tasks without interaction. The definition and the behavior of a subject depend on the order of sent and received messages, tasks being accomplished and the way in which it influences the behavior.

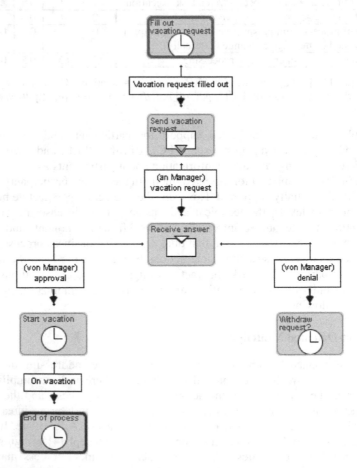

Fig. 1. Applying for holidays – behavior specification of the subject Employee

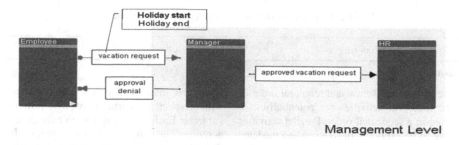

Fig. 2. Message exchange between the subject Employee and Management Level

If a subject sends a message the information transferred with that message is derived from user inputs or computed by some applications. These 'send' functions are executed before a message is sent. Vice versa, once a subject accepts a message a corresponding function is executed. The information received through the message is used as input for that function. This type of functions represent so-called refinements of a subject. They constitute the interface of a subject to the applications utilized by the subject.

3 Subject-Specific Task Accomplishment

Before detailing the flow of control for subject-oriented modeling and execution of work tasks and business processes we contrast the approach to strict flow-oriented specification schemes in section 3.1, as concepts from flow-oriented modeling have influenced the design of subject/message-driven control (section 3.2).

3.1 Actor-Specific Flow of Control

In order to compare flow-oriented modeling to the subject-oriented approach fundamental concepts including the relationship to organizational structures have to be clarified. Besides documentation referring to representational issues, such as granularity, interfacing, and the way of abstraction for high-level (cross-) organizational processes are detailed in the comparison. Finally, with respect to execution simulation and exception handling are detailed for each type of approach.

The comparison reveals for subject-driven process specification a strict orientation towards actors and messages. It enables straightforward implementation due to the coherent flow specification. However, an overall top-down specification, e.g., starting with a (highly abstract) value chain that is successively refined to processes, is not possible using this approach. Such a perspective has been given up for the sake of task-complete specification.

3.2 Subject-Driven Flow of Control

The flow of control in a networked subject-driven environment can be best illustrated proceeding with the vacation process example. The behavior of the manager is complementary to the employee's. The messages sent by employees are received by the

Table 2. Contrasting flow-orientation to subject-orientation

Flow-oriented Modeling	Subject-oriented Modeling
Concept	
Focus on control flow and temporal order of activities: All activities are potentially executed in a sequential order. Parallel activities have to be explicitly introduced and modeled via fork and join operators. The main modeling elements are activities (or process steps) and the control flow between the steps.	Focus on internal activities and behavior with respect to partners of the various subjects: Each subject is able to execute its activities in parallel to each other. If activities require synchronization between subjects, it has to be modeled explicitly. The main modeling elements are subjects, their internal behavior and their message exchange.
Relationship to organizational structure	
The organizational structure of a company can be modeled independently of processes. The relationship between the organizational structure and processes is established by assigning roles or organizational units to process steps. It is not possible to show the flow of a process through the functional structure of an organization.	The organizational structure of a company can be modeled independently of its work processes. The relationship between the organizational structure and the processes is established by assigning subjects to organizational units or roles. The workflow represents the organizational structure.
Overall or cross-organizational Process Representation	
The "big picture" of a process (value chain of a company) based on detailed process descriptions can be created. It shows all process steps on a high level of abstraction including the involved resources, mostly to create a management- and network-partner view on a process.	A high-level view on the process representing the contribution of each participant requires abstraction, since each subject is only related to its adjacent interaction partners.
Interfaces between processes / Sub processes	
Interfaces between processes are handled by events and activities. A specific activity in a specific process triggers the starting activity in another process, expressed by events.	Interfaces between processes are handled by subjects: A subject belonging to one process sends a message to a subject belonging to another process, in order to start a sub process or trigger a follow-up process.
Process Abstraction	
Process abstraction allows refining a high-level model to a detailed specification of (certain parts of) the model. Objects of refinement are process steps. In each level of abstraction certain process steps are detailed.	Work-process abstraction means refining a high level model to a detailed specification (of certain parts) of the model. Object of refinement are subjects. Refinements exist on the level of subjects, interactions, and internal behavior specifications of subjects.

Table 2. (*continued*)

Process Visibility / Transparency	
Concepts like views allow for distinct process visibility. Each participant of a process (subject) is able to specify an externally visible representation of the internal process flow. It is achieved through combining different tasks to a view. In this way, the relationship of external and internal steps is specified, and monitoring at runtime can be performed on active instances.	For each subject an externally visible specification (interface) of its internal behavior can be created. The same holds for a complete process. There is no dedicated relationship of internal tasks to their external representation.
Exception Modeling	
Exceptions have to be modeled as part of the overall flow of control. Each exception has to be positioned through analyzing its possible occurrences. Mechanisms have to be introduced to capture the corresponding events for active exception handling.	Exceptions are subject-specific. Due to the likely high rate of running processes in parallel, exception handling becomes less complicated compared to flow-oriented modeling. When subjects are in a waiting state they can handle either the standard flow of work, or incoming exceptions.
Execution Architecture	
The flow-oriented approach suggests the use of a single execution engine, as the flow of control is not specified for each subject separately.	The subject-oriented flow suggests the use of separate engines for each subject. However, the respective decision lies beyond the process specification (availability, trust, contract etc.).
Simulation	
Processes can be simulated in terms of the logical control flow. An end-to-end simulation of the overall process can be performed, showing the sequence of process steps (work tasks). This enables the validation of the overall process ("big picture"). However, the view cannot be restricted to the contribution of a single subject.	Processes can be simulated from the point of view of each subject. The internal behavior, the data exchanged and the external communication are considered explicitly. Each subject recognizes its contribution to the process, but not the overall picture in terms of concatenated value chain elements representing core processes of the organization.

manager and vice versa. Figure 3 shows the behavior of the manager. The manager is on hold for the holiday application of the employee. Upon receipt the holiday application is checked (state). This check can either result in an approval or a rejection, leading to either state, informing the employee. In case the holiday application is approved, the HR department is informed about the successful application.

In order to complete the process the behavior of the HR department needs to be detailed. It receives the approved holiday application and puts it to the employee's days-off record, without further activities (process completion).

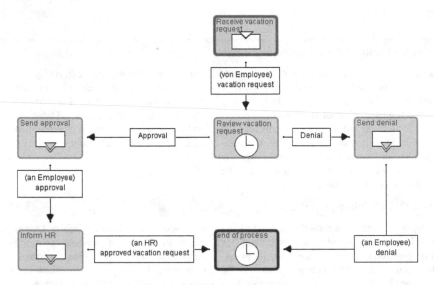

Fig. 3. Behavior specification of Manager in the holiday application process

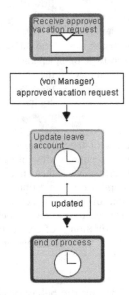

Fig. 4. HR department behavioral response to approved vacation requests

The description of a subject defines the sequence of sending and receiving messages or the processing of internal functions, respectively. In this way, a subject specification contains the pushing sequence of functions, so-called services (as an abstraction from implementation). These services can be the standard ones like 'send' and 'receive', or predicates dealing with specific objects, such as required when an employee files a vacation request (see also Figure 2). Consequently, each node (state) and transition has to be assigned to an operation. The implementation of that operation does not matter at that stage, since it can be handled by object specifications, as shown in the implementation section.

A service is assigned to an internal, functional node of a subject. Once this state is reached, the assigned service is triggered and processed. The end conditions correspond to links leaving the internal functional node. Each result link of a sending node (state) is assigned to a named service. Before sending, this service is triggered to identify the content or parameter of a message. The service determines the values of the message parameters transferred by the message. Analogously, each output link of a receiving node (state) is also assigned to a named service. When accepting a message in the receive state, that service is triggered to identify the parameter of the received message. The service determines the values of the parameters transferred by the message and prepares them for further processing.

As services are used to assign a certain meaning to each work step in a subject, they allow defining the functions of a subject. All of those are triggered in a synchronous way, i.e. a subject only reaches its subsequent state once all triggered services have been completed. Figure 5 shows how the functions of a subject are defined by means of objects. In this way, a process specification can be completed for automated execution.

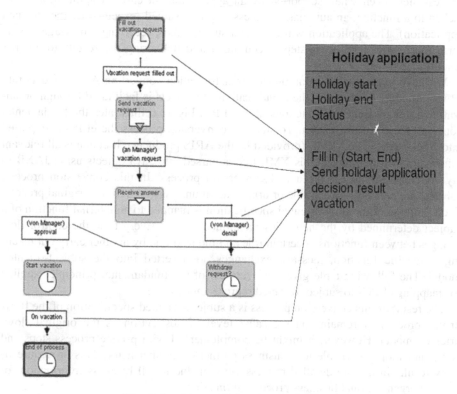

Fig. 5. A subject with functions and objects

4 Transformation and Execution

As we cannot expect organizations to rewrite their business process specifications or to switch from a flow- or function-oriented, top-down to a subject- or actor-oriented, bottom-up modeling approach, existing models need to be converted. We exemplify such a conversion for the most commonly used ARIS approach in section 4.1. In section 4.2 we briefly detail the execution of the (transformed) process representations.

4.1 From ARIS to jPASS! – Automated Model Transformation

For a consistent automated model transformation from flow-oriented to subject-oriented approaches the flow-oriented model requires information with respect to organizational and operational resources. A resource may be a role, an organizational unit or a system, attached to a function in a flow-oriented model. If more than one of the named resource types is attached to a function, a decision has to be made to which subject (the human or the system subject) this function should be assigned. In general, the human subject is the preferred one, as usually a person has the leading part in a process step, even when supported by an application. In case an application is attached to a function, an automated process step is assumed (executed by the attached application). The application will act like a subject, thus, receiving a message to perform the respective process step, executing it and delivering the results to another resource.

We have implemented an automated transformation converting ARIS models into jPASS! models. In this case the identification of subjects is facilitated through organizational units attached to functions of an eEPC. Figure 6 illustrates the fundamental concept of the transformation. To start the conversion process the eEPC is exported into AML, a dedicated XML (provided by the ARIS producer). It contains all relevant information of the model. This XML tree is parsed into Java objects using JAXB to lay coherent ground for the actual conversion process. In this conversion process, subjects are created for each role or organization unit, as given in the original process. Each function of the flow-oriented specification is mapped to an internal function of a subject determined by the heuristics mentioned before. Every time the control flow changes between functions, a certain role and the next one by another carry out meaning a specific function, message exchanges are inserted into the subject-oriented model. The following table gives an overview of the fundamental principles applied for mapping eEPCs to subject-oriented representations.

The result of this conversion process is a subject-oriented specification of the flow-driven process. It remains on the same level of abstraction as the original flow-oriented model. However, it might be complemented with private process steps and communication not visible to a business partner or another actor. This procedure finally results in a more detailed process view, including all business information for (cross-) organizational business process automation.

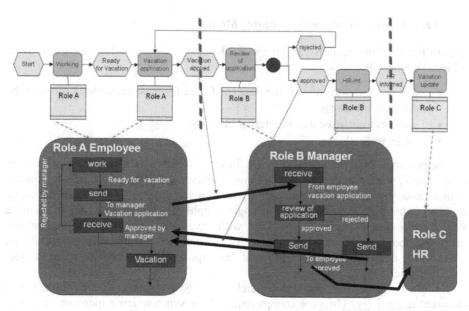

Fig. 6. Mapping a sample ARIS specification to subjects

Table 2. Transformation principles when mapping eEPCs to subject-oriented models

eEPC	Subject-oriented model	Details
Organizational unit attached to an action	Subject	For the subject the same name as for the organizational unit can be used.
System attached to an action	Subject	Systems / Applications are considered as automated subjects.
Action	Internal function of the corresponding subject	An organizational unit or a subject executing the corresponding action is attached.
Event between actions with the same organizational unit attached	Result of the internal action preceding the event	Succeeding actions with the same organizational unit attached are executed in the same subject.
Event between actions with different organizational units attached	A message with the same name as the event from the subject representing the organizational unit assigned to the action preceding the event to the subject representing the organizational unit assigned to the succeeding action.	In case of different organizational units attached to succeeding actions, the organizational unit assigned to the first action has to inform the organizational unit assigned to the following action, so that the succeeding action can be executed.

4.2 Transformation into an Executable Model

Before the resulting models can be executed, some technical information has to be added. This includes

- a detailed description of the data (and data formats) exchanged through the different messages
- services to be executed in internal functions
- target technologies.

As the requirements for the execution of different tasks in a process may differ from case to case, it is necessary to be able to map different tasks to different technologies. While tasks that do not require user interaction but fast processing can easily be mapped onto a BPEL-based workflow engine, highly interactive tasks might be more suited for a web application combined with Java code. This type of applications allows embedding human interactions or human interventions into workflows, whereas for BPEL applications additional development effort has to be spent to meet this objective.

Using a subject-oriented process model it is possible to execute each subject on a different technology. The time stamps required for synchronizing message exchange are already part of the internal process description of each subject, and the data exchanged is already part of the specified messages. In order to enable this synchronization a protocol or "lingua franca", such as a web service technology, has to be used that can be processed by the technologies involved.

5 Conclusion

Subject-oriented development of organizations or networks of processes overcomes deficiencies of traditional approaches. As the latter focus on structuring content and/or specifying business logic and task models in a top-down fashion, they hardly provide a dedicated communication scheme. Such schemes describing the synchronization for actors are crucial, since the mapping of work-task models to coding schemes or software architectures might lack coherence in case of incomplete flow specifications.

The presented formation of processes based on the communication among actors (subjects) does not only ensure coherence of workflows, but also allows for semantically adequate representations at the task level. Consequently, these representations can be directly used for implementation and automated execution.

The corresponding tool jPASS! (see also [12] and http://www.jcom1.com) facilitates the accurate formation of organizations and their networks based on actual work processes, as it enables the immediate execution of subject-oriented specifications. Moreover, existing process specifications, such as ARIS [11] might be transformed to subject-oriented ones automatically using dedicated mark-up languages. The resulting workflow execution might either run on existing engines, or require accustomed service architectures.

Our upcoming research activities will concern the handling of different levels of detail/abstraction when organizations are networked to handle common business opportunities. The tuning and mapping of different levels of granularity is still an open issue, even when subjects can be identified handling business objects. Topics, such as the propagation of encapsulated information and synchronization, have priority on our research agenda. The running European R&D project SUDDEN (www.sudden.biz) allows us to work with industry partners to that respect. This is challenging, as they emerge as service providers from traditional producers in dynamic supply and engineering networks.

References

1. Chakraborthy, D.: Extending the reach of business processes. IEEE Computer 37(4), 78–80 (2004)
2. Davenport, T.H.: Process innovation: reengineering work through information technology, Boston, Mass. (1993)
3. Ehrig, M.: Ontology alignment. Bridging the semantic gap. Springer, Berlin (2007)
4. Fleischmann, A.: Distributed systems. Software design & implementation. Springer, Berlin (1994)
5. Haeckel, S.S.: Adaptive enterprise: Creating and leading sense-AND-respond organizations. Harvard Business School Press, Cambridge (1999)
6. Havey, M.: Essential Business Process Modeling. O'Reilly, Beijing (2005)
7. Laudon, K.-C., Laudon, J.P.: Essentials of management information systems: Managing the digital firm, 6th edn. Pearson, Upper Saddle River (2005)
8. Lewis, M., Young, B., Mathiassen, L., Rai, A., Welke, R.: Business process innovation based on stakeholder perceptions. Information Knowledge Systems Management 6, 7–17 (2007)
9. Lippe, S., Greiner, U., Barros, A.: A Survey on State-of-the-Art to facilitate modelling of cross-organisational business processes. In: Proc. of XML4BPM 2005, Karlsruhe (2005)
10. Rouse, W.B. (ed.): Enterprise transformation: Understanding and enabling fundamental change. Wiley, Hoboken (2006)
11. Scheer, A.-W.: ARIS - Modellierungsmethoden, Metamodelle, Anwendungen, 4th edn. Springer, Berlin (2001)
12. Schmidt, W., Fleischmann, A., Gilbert, O.: Subjektorientiertes Geschäfts-prozessmanagement. HMD Praxis der Wirtschaftsinformatik (April 2009); English version can be obtained from albert.fleischmann@jcom1.com
13. Stary, C.: TADEUS: Seamless development of task-based and user-oriented interfaces. IEEE Transactions on Systems, Man, and Cybernetics, Part A 30(5), 509–525 (2000)
14. Stephenson, S.V., Sage, A.: Architecting for enterprise resource planning. Information Knowledge Systems Management 6, 81–121 (2007)
15. Strosnider, J.K., Nandi, P., Kumaran, S., Ghosh, S., Arsanjani, A.: Model-driven synthesis of SOA solutions. IBM Systems Journal 47(3), 415–423 (2008)

Weighting Task Procedure for Zoomable Task Hierarchy Modeling of Rich Internet Applications

Francisco J. Martínez-Ruiz[1], Jean Vanderdonckt[1], and Jaime Muñoz[2]

[1] Université catholique de Louvain, Belgian Lab. of Computer-Human Interaction
Place des Doyens, 1 – B-1348 Louvain-la-Neuve, Belgium
{francisco.martinez,jean.vanderdonckt}@uclouvain.be
[2] Universidad Autónoma de Aguascalientes, México
jmunozar@correo.uaa.mx

Abstract. Zoomable user interfaces are more attractive because they offer the possibility to present information and to support actions according to a "focus+context" method: while a context of use is preserved or presented in a more compact way, the focus can be achieved on some part of the information and actions, enabling the end user to focus on one part at a time. While this interaction technique can be straightforwardly applied for manipulating objects of the same type (e.g., cells in a spreadsheet or appointments in a calendar), it is less obvious how to present interactive tasks of an information system where tasks may involve very different amount and types of information and actions. For this purpose, this paper introduces a metric based on a task model in order to decide what portion of a task model should lead to a particular user interface container, group, or fragment, while preserving the task structure. Each branch of the task model is assigned to a weight that will lead to such a container, group, or fragment depending on parameters computed on variables belonging to the context of use. In this way, not only the task structure is preserved, but also the decomposition of the user interface into elements depends on the context of use, particularly the constraints imposed by the computing platform.

Keywords: Multiple contexts of use, Rich Internet Applications, Task-based metric, Task Tree modeling, Task weighting, Task coding schemes.

1 Introduction

The task model has been widely recognized as a rich source for initiating the development life cycle of a User Interface (UI) of an interactive system [27]. When it comes to designing a UI for multiple contexts of use, for instance on different computing platforms, the task model has also been exploited in order to drive the process of deciding how the UI will be decomposed into screens and how the transition between these screens will be ensured. This paper tackles a specific necessity of the first step in the method proposed in [5] which was conceived as a Model Driven approach for the developing Rich Internet Applications (RIAs): How to calculate (and justify) the weight of task Hierarchies?

D. England et al. (Eds.): TAMODIA 2009, LNCS 5963, pp. 92–102, 2010.
© Springer-Verlag Berlin Heidelberg 2010

This initial task is the specification of user goals as a task hierarchy, i.e., a task hierarchy model of the application (THM). The procedure is indeed an iterative process, beginning with general tasks which are decomposed into simpler tasks. This work produces structures of variable size (for non-trivial developments the caliber increase very quick). The specification in the previous version of the method is based on ConcurTaskTree notation [15]. One of the drawbacks of this notation is the visual ambiguity. That is, the repetitive structures which conforms them are not prepared to help in the process of pattern recovery or semantic inferences. In order to resolve this problematic, The Zoomable User Interface (ZUIT) is used. For instance, this alternative visualization can help developers to: (1) Finding hidden patterns and (2) Identifying unbalanced hierarchies (i.e., putting many tasks in a sub tree) which intuitively implies a poor UI design.

The rest of this paper is organized as follows: Section 2 discuss the state of the art in the creation of ZUIs. Section 3 introduces the reference framework. Then Section 4 covers the description of our method over a minimalistic case study. In Section 5, another example is presented. And finally, Section 6 presents conclusions and future work.

2 Related Work and Problem Description

This section includes three subsections: first, a brief review of the state of the art in the domain of RIAs. Second, one dedicated to Zoomable User Interfaces. And third, an analysis of the problem in terms of weight measure.

2.1 RIA Complexity

The complexity of RIA applications involves multiple factors. First, there are a lot of elements to coordinate in order to model the UI presentation. Second, they include unusual widgets with nontraditional behavior. Third, the web page metaphor is not maintained. That is, reloading of web pages is substituted by a continuously present interface with soft transitions [5], [17].

2.2 Review of Zoomable User Interfaces

The selection of Zoomable user interfaces (ZUI) is based on the benefits that could afford to RIA development. For instance, searching information in schematic diagrams [10]. ZUIs are suitable for dealing with hierarchical structures (e.g., images or 3D scenarios) and vast sets of information [3]. In [9] 2D structures were used in order to display the internal disposition of files in a directory structure of hard disks. Note: Here instead of dealing with files of variable size we have tasks with different complexities. Also, in [10] one of the contributions of ZUIs is the sense of location combined with object constancy (i.e., I could browse the THM without losing resolution and sense of location). In [7] and [14] the advantages of ZUIs in comparison to window based ones are studied. It is possible to find interesting examples: a calendar application for mobile devices that combines fisheye views with reduced overviews [12]. Another example is a time-line with zooming facilities [13]. The development of this kind of applications does not follow a model driven approach.

2.3 Problem Description

In [5] the first step of development includes THMs as the initial phase. But the used THMs are weightless structures and there is a lack of sense of complexity. RIAs are very complex and the developer needs support in the moment of designing the definition of the application in terms of THMs. Therefore, the objective of this research is proposing a weighting process in order to produce more balanced structures. The sub goals of this include (A) a weighting function that takes into account the structure (locally and globally). (B) The structure could aid to discover easily overloaded sections of the application. (C) Providing a plausible alternative to current THM solutions in terms of efficient space utilization and interactivity (thanks to the ZUI approach). Finally, it is worth to mention that building task models [15] is not a trivial task. Even with the inclusion of limited zooming of some tree branches, word wrapping and fisheye treatment [23], the visualization (e.g., labels) and complexity description problems remain unresolved.

3 Alignment with the CAMALEON Reference Framework

In order to give a self contained presentation of the method, in the following section is briefly reviewed and after that, the focus of this paper is retaken. The method proposed in [5] uses as building scheme, the CAMELEON framework [24] and includes as first step the definition of a task hierarchy model or task tree (THM) in order to describe User goals (this level is called Task and Domain level). This model is then transformed into an abstract definition, called AUI and then to a concrete one, called CUI. Here, modality and type of widget selection are completed. Then, the last transformation is done. This Final UI is built in a specific platform (LZX, .NET, SWF among others). Note: it is a Model Driven compliant method as defined by OMG [16].

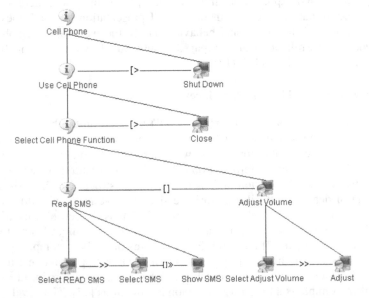

Fig. 1. Example of THM of some functionalities of a cell phone

3.1 Generating the Alternative Representation of Task Model

ZUIT representation of THMs uses a constant display area in order to show THMs of any size. The THM is traversed in a breadth-first order (see Fig. 3) and the transformation process is completed by XSL templates. The ZUIT definition includes two steps. (1) The weight-less ZUIT is first created (see Fig. 2). Here the inner boxes are spread in a regular order. That is, they take all available space like HTML table cells. And (2) each cell is updated in order to represent in a better way the complexity of the application (see section 4). In Fig. 1, we could see an example of a THM for describing some functions of a cell phone (adapted from [27]).

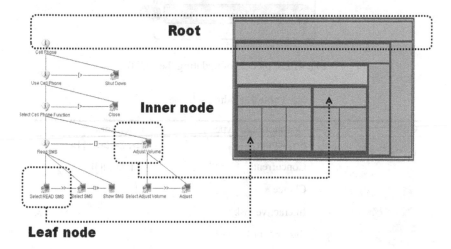

Fig. 2. Transformation of THM into ZUIT format

```
Function CreateZUIT structure(CTT tree)
returns ZuiStructure or failure
initialize the search tree to root node
loop do
      if there are no candidate nodes for expansion
      then return exit
      choose a node and expand its sons
            if node type equals parent-node then
                  GeneratBoxComponent()
            if node type equals leaf-node then
                  GeneratCellComponent()
                  DefineContainmentRelation(leaf, parent)
```

Fig. 3. A possible algorithm for generating the ZUIT structure

4 Method Outline

The following section describes the proposed refinements in order to calculate the weight (see Figure 4). A first step is the replacement of textual definitions by a color

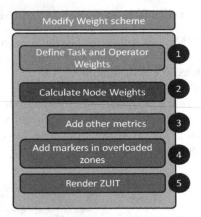

Fig. 4. The process of updating the ZUIT

Table 1. Coding scheme

Color	Operator/task Type	Operators
	Sequential	[>, |>, >>, []>>
	Concurrent	|=|, ||| , |[]|
	Choice	[]
	Interactive task	
	System task	
	Abstract task	

coding scheme in order to deliver visually simpler THMs (since it is not practical to deal with hundreds of labels). Also, the temporal operators are coded in colored headers which meaning could be seen in table 1.

The application of this process could be seen in Fig. 5. This process is done with the purpose of reducing the cognitive overload of the developer. Note: in order to make clearer the explanation, task names are included in Fig. 5 but in the real ZUIT task labels are included only as tool tips.

4.1 Definition of Task and Temporal Operator Costs

The complexity of each task is expressed with a specific weight (or cost). That is, the weight of each sub THM is directly proportional its complexity. The cost of each type is defined with an exponential growth function, $y = 2^n$ where n is a value between one and three. The rationale behind this selection includes two empirical reasons: (1) the minimal THM involves two tasks which give us the Base and (2) Sequential temporal operators involve one active task at a given time, so they have the lower cost. A choice operator before the selection involves more complexity but after

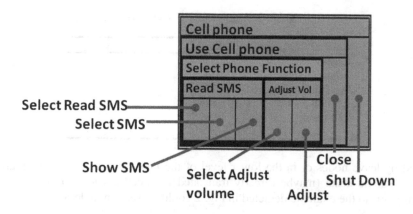

Fig. 5. ZUIT representation of some cell phone operations

the selection only one way is taken. Finally, concurrent operators imply execution in parallel, and then their cost is the biggest. Note: These weights were proposed in [17]. Meanwhile, the task types are also based in terms of the same logic: an application task is simpler (always from the UI perspective since is an output process in most of the cases) than an interactive task which implies a dialogue. Then, the second doubles the first in terms of cost (see table 2).

Table 2. Weight of THM elements

Weight	Task Type	Operator type
8	-	Concurrent
4	Interactive	Choice
2	Application	Sequence

4.2 Calculate Node Weights

The following function (1) is proposed in order to produce node weights.

$$W = \frac{n}{2}\left(\frac{\sum_{i=1}^{n} T_i \times TaskWeight + \sum_{j=1}^{m} O_j \times OpWeight}{deep}\right) \qquad (1)$$

Where, **n** is the number of tasks in the sub tree, the division by two is related with the size of the minimal possible tree, i.e. the weight is understood as proportional increments of the weight of the minimal tree. **T** is the set of task nodes and/or head nodes of sub trees that are part of the current sub tree. **O** is the set of operators in the current level. Note: m= n-1, also for the sake of simplicity, we assume only a single temporal operator type in the case of different types, dummy tasks are created to cover and send them down. **Deep** is the distance from the root to the set of nodes to be weighted, the rationale behind the introduction of this value is to reduce the weight of sub trees

Table 3. Weight of ZUIT elements

Abstract Container	Weight
Read SMS	5,25
Adjust Volume	2,5
Select phone function	7,75
Use cell phone	6,875
Cell phone	12,875

formed by leave nodes or in the lower level of the task hierarchy, since they are related to simple tasks (maybe directly translated to specific widgets). The result of applying this to the example depicted in Fig. 2 could be seen in table 3.

4.3 Add Other Metrics

Other metrics could be added in order to refine the weighting process. For instance, centrality (CE) is a plausible one since introduce a notion of weight in terms of local and global position of tasks [25]. This metric takes into account the connectedness of a node. The rationale behind this metric is that inner nodes ranked with a considerable centrality value are the head of complex sub hierarchies.

4.4 Add Markers in Overloaded Zones

Another automatic process to be included is the control of overloaded areas. For instance, in Fig. 6a the number of children tasks is more than seven (indeed, there are fourteen tasks) and according to [26] this is not suitable (this value is used here in order to introduce a known capacity value). Then, the header's color is changed to red (see Fig. 6b). And there is a possible mechanical solution of subdividing the task into subtasks up to a specific capacity value. In Fig. 6c, the capacity is established to seven and Fig. 6d takes remaining tasks. Also more complicated algorithms could be introduced. For instance the one proposed in [28] but it requires adding more info about tasks and their translation to specific widgets and contexts.

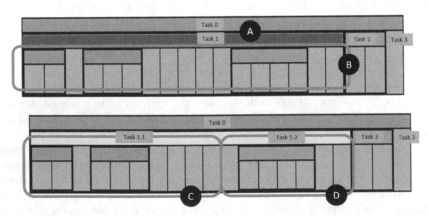

Fig. 6. Zooming process of the ZUIT for using a cell phone

4.5 Render the ZUIT

The process of rendering is done with the PICCOLO library [19]. The hierarchy of nodes is rendered into 2D graphical elements with the proper area and it could be navigated through zooming in and out operations (see Fig. 7).

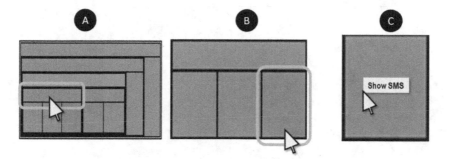

Fig. 7. Zooming process of the ZUIT for using a cell phone

5 Other Example: Cocktail Selection Application

In this section another example is presented. This application is used to select cocktails (see Fig. 8) also combines Zoomable capabilities with the expression of the ZUIs (here in gray scale in Fig. 9). Also we show here a possible THM (see Fig. 10).

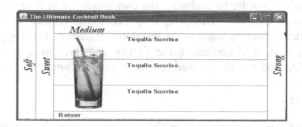

Fig. 8. Cocktail selection application

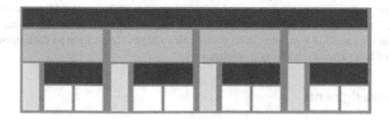

Fig. 9. Cocktail ZUIT representation

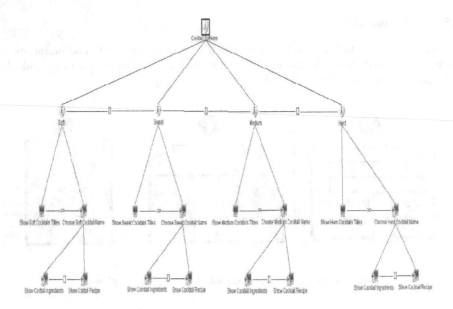

Fig. 10. Cocktail typical THM representation

6 Conclusions and Directions for Future Research

In this paper we introduce an updated weighing procedure (with the proposition of a weighting formula) in order to deal with the complexity of different task hierarchies in the development of RIAs. This weighting process is applied in Zoomable User Interfaces in order to surpass some of the problems of current THM approach. Piccolo framework [19] is used to implement the ZUITs. Finally, this approach is not only applicable to RIAs and it could be used for others types of applications.

6.1 Future Work

Only a couple of metrics were used in this first version of the function but we are introducing more metrics as these would continue to move our approach to its goal of being a known alternative representation of task models. In the meantime, a piccolo prototype is under construction in order to test the feasibility and adding more capabilities. Finally, more semantic exploration and elements could be added to our representation e.g., usability weights in terms of color ranges (from light to dark in order to represent adherence to usability guidelines).

Acknowledgments

This work is supported by the Programme AlBan, the European Union Programme of High Level Scholarships for Latin America, scholarship No. (E06D101371MX) and the Belgian Computer Human Interaction Lab.

References

1. Dachselt, R., Frisch, M.: Mambo: a facet-based zoomable music browser. In: Proceedings of the 6th international Conference on Mobile and Ubiquitous Multimedia, MUM 2007, Oulu, December 12-14, vol. 284, pp. 110–117. ACM, New York (2007)
2. Dachselt, R., Frisch, M., Weiland, M.: FacetZoom: a continuous multi-scale widget for navigating hierarchical metadata. In: Proceeding of the Twenty-Sixth Annual SIGCHI Conference on Human Factors in Computing Systems, CHI 2008, Florence, Italy, April 5-10, pp. 1353–1356. ACM, New York (2008)
3. Plumlee, M.D., Ware, C.: Zooming versus multiple window interfaces: Cognitive costs of visual comparisons. ACM Trans. Comput.-Hum. Interact. 13(2), 179–209 (2006)
4. UsiXML (January 15, 2007), http://www.usixml.org/
5. Martínez-Ruiz, F.J., Muñoz Arteaga, J., Vanderdonckt, J., González-Calleros, J.M.: A first draft of a Model-driven Method for Designing Graphical User Interfaces of Rich Internet Applications. In: Proc. of 4th Latin American Web Congress LA-Web 2006, Puebla, October 25-27. IEEE Computer Society Press, Los Alamitos (2006)
6. Bederson, B.B., Meyer, J., Good, L.: Jazz: an extensible zoomable user interface graphics toolkit in Java. In: Proceedings of the 13th Annual ACM Symposium on User interface Software and Technology, UIST 2000, San Diego, Cal., United States, November 6-8. ACM, New York (2000)
7. Combs, T.T., Bederson, B.B.: Does zooming improve image browsing? In: Proceedings of the Fourth ACM Conference on Digital Libraries, DL 1999, Berkeley, California, August 11-14, pp. 130–137. ACM, New York (1999)
8. Furnas, G.W., Zhang, X.: MuSE: a multiscale editor. In: Proc. of the 11th Annual ACM Symposium on User interface Software and Technology, UIST 1998, San Francisco, November 1-4, pp. 107–116. ACM, New York (1998)
9. Johnson, B., Shneiderman, B.: Tree-Maps: a space-filling approach to the visualization of hierarchical information structures. In: Nielson, G.M., Rosenblum, L. (eds.) Proceedings of the 2nd Conference on Visualization 1991, IEEE Visualization, San Diego, Cal., October 22 - 25. IEEE Computer Soc. Press, Los Alamitos (1991)
10. Perlin, K., Meyer, J.: Nested user interface components. In: Proceedings of the 12th Annual ACM Symposium on User interface Software and Technology, UIST 1999, Asheville, North Carolina, USA, November 7-10, pp. 11–18. ACM, New York (1999)
11. Appert, C., Fekete, J.: OrthoZoom scroller: 1D multi-scale navigation. In: Proc. CHI 2006, pp. 21–30. ACM Press, New York (2006)
12. Bederson, B.B., Clamage, A., Czerwinski, M.P., Robertson, G.G.: DateLens: A fisheye calendar interface for PDAs. Transactions on Computer-Human Interaction 11(1), 90–119 (2004)
13. Dachselt, R., Weiland, M.: TimeZoom: a flexible detail and context timeline. In: CHI 2006 Extended Abstracts, pp. 682–687. ACM Press, New York (2006)
14. Bederson, B., Boltman, A.: Does Animation Help Users Build Mental Maps of Spatial Information. Submitted to CHI 1999 (1999)
15. Paternò, F.: Towards a UML for Interactive Systems. In: Nigay, L., Little, M.R. (eds.) EHCI 2001. LNCS, vol. 2254, p. 7. Springer, Heidelberg (2001)
16. OMG, http://www.omg.org (May 10, 2009)
17. Martinez-Ruiz, F.J., Vanderdonckt, J., Arteaga, J.M.: Context-aware Generation of User Interface Containers for a Mobil Device. In: Mexican International Conferences on Computer Science, IEEE track in Human-Computer Interaction, Mexico, October 2008, pp. 63–72 (2008)

18. http://www.nespresso.com (May 10, 2009)
19. http://www.piccolo2d.org (May 10, 2009)
20. Montero, F., López-Jaquero, V., Lozano, M., González, P.: IdealXML: un entorno para la gestión de experiencia relacionada con el desarrollo hipermedial. In: ADACO: Ing. de la usabilidad en nuevos paradigmas aplicados a entornos web colaborativos y adaptativos, Proy. Cicyt TEN2004-08000-C03-03, Granada (September 2005)
21. Martinez-Ruiz, F.: A Development Method for User Interfaces of Rich Internet Applications, DEA thesis, UCL, Louvain-la-Neuve, August 31 (2007)
22. http://jquery.com (May 10, 2009)
23. Paternò, F., Zini, E.: Applying information visualization techniques to visual representations of task models. In: Proc. of the 3rd Annual Conf. on Task Models and Diagrams, TAMODIA 2004, Prague, November 15-16, vol. 86. ACM, New York (2004)
24. Calvary, G., Coutaz, J., Thevenin, D., Limbourg, Q., Bouillon, L., Vanderdonckt, J.: A Unifying Reference Framework for Multi-Target User Interfaces. Interacting with Comp. 15(3), 289–308 (2003)
25. Dhyani, D., Ng, W.K., Bhowmick, S.S.: A survey of Web metrics. ACM Comput. Surv. 34(4), 469–503 (2002)
26. Miller, G.A.: The magical number seven, plus or minus two: Some limits on our capacity for processing information. Psychological Review 63, 81–97 (1956)
27. Luyten, K., Clerckx, T., Coninx, K., Vanderdonckt, J.M.: Derivation of a Dialog Model from a Task Model by Activity Chain Extraction. In: Jorge, J.A., Nunes, N.J., Cunha, J.F.e. (eds.) Proceedings of the 8th International Workshop on Interactive Systems: Design, Specification, and Verification, Funchal, Madeira Island, Portugal, June 11-13, pp. 203–217 (2003)
28. Chu, H., Song, H., Wong, C., Kurakake, S., Katagiri, M.: Roam, a seamless application framework. J. Syst. Softw. 69(3) (January 2004)

Task Modelling Using Situation Calculus

Martin Randles, David England, and A. Taleb-Bendiab

School of Computing and Mathematical Sciences, Liverpool John Moores University,
Liverpool, UK
{m.j.randles,d.england,a.talebbendiab}@ljmu.ac.uk

Abstract. The main aim of this paper is to demonstrate the effectiveness of using Situation Calculus in Task Modelling. The motivation for this approach is to enable a runtime adaptable task model to be used in the provision of the most appropriate user interfaces, according to circumstance. The task model and meta-reasoning model may both be specfied in the Situation Calculus, which permits reasoning to occur over couterfactual situations and without exhaustive state enumeration. A task flow editor with input from the formal model is demonstrated and the approach is described using a medical process case study.

Keywords: Situation calculus, Task modelling.

1 Introduction

Task driven computing is an established paradigm for pervasive computing, where users can access and manipulate information from anywhere at any time based on task analysis [1]: Middleware services autonomously provide a context for specific tasks across multiple devices transparently to the user. In modelling user interfaces, to be adaptive to individual or environmental requirements, it is likewise necessary to consider task models, which may be adapted at run time to the most appropriate form. It is envisaged, in this paper, that middleware services will provide facilities to observe and deliberate on task models to provide an awareness of the system and its environment. A user interface may thus be presented that most accurately represents the current circumstances and available options, to the user, anywhere at any time: Permitting the exhibition of adaptability; the system is capable of user customisation, and adaptivity; the system automatically adapts to the perceived situation [2].

The usual design of user interfaces most often occurs in response to a preconceived notion of the systems' functions and likely user requirements. As complexity increases, however, it becomes increasingly difficult, if not impossible, to implement user interfaces through the hard coding of all the requirements for adaptation to the user's situation. The work reported on here is seeking to use task modelling for matching users' specific contexts (device type and capabilities, location, interaction style, etc) to the underlying functional systems: It is proposed to use an established layered observation system [3] with a formal logical task model in Situation Calculus [4]. The Situation Calculus has been used, more recently, as a calculus of situations marking a distinction from the original setting of McCarthy and Hayes [5]. It offers a flexible formalism in which to reason about dynamic systems.

D. England et al. (Eds.): TAMODIA 2009, LNCS 5963, pp. 103–116, 2010.
© Springer-Verlag Berlin Heidelberg 2010

In this instance Situation Calculus is, in effect, presented as a task modelling language, for both meta-system and system tasks, uniquely able to handle counterfactual reasoning, for deliberation on context to produce a deployable user interaction task model that can be modified and updated at run time. Furthermore this Situation Calculus task model serves as an input for a task based flow model in a developed task flow editor for analysis and modification of the formal task model and code generation. For example the location of an employee in a work place directly impacts on the task model and the associated cognitive attributes of the context (the intentions or goals of a task will vary according to context). Thus the cognitive aspects of any offered user interface need to be considered. In this instance a logical representation of the domain permits intention reconsideration based on an employee's location and deliberation, using couterfactual reasoning, on the task models and subsequent interface options.

The research presented in this paper is founded on the Background and Related Works detailed in Section 2. Section 3 provides a more thorough account of the Situation Calculus and its applicability, whilst section 4 gives an overview of the task flow editor and its workings. Section 5 reports on the application of these techniques to a real world clinical based case study, where task (or decision) models are adapted according to the context (situation) of the doctor (or other autheticated system user). The paper finishes with a conclusion and suggested further work in Section 6.

2 Background and Related Works

The context and situation is considered, in this paper, as an extremely important aspect of task modelling for user interface production. Despite established definitions offereing a wide scope for context [6], very few approaches account for both the physical and cognitive context of users [7]: Either the users' physical locations are considered for proximity to resources, etc. [8] or the users' preferences or goals are used to give a context [9]; very rarely is a more complete account presented encompassing both the physical and mental states of the user. The modelling solution presented here allows the adaptation of task models based on a more complete user environmental and cognitive context. This is achieved through a logical representation of the task model and a meta-task model for deliberation on the tasks. In this way task context can be deduced using, for example, user preference in line with domain constraints, handling the trade-off between user autonomy and systems governance [10]. Currently design models for user interface task models do not employ "cognitive" (including deliberative independent) behaviour to support in-situ autonomy, but rather use explicitly managed autonomy via policies and rule sets that predefine and predict all extraneous behaviour specified at design time often using Event Condition Action (ECA) constructs [11]. Whilst, this is a well tested and understood design principle the authors argue that often this has limited reach when applied to open, ad-hoc and evolving software systems. Thus, in this paper we outline a task modelling approach for adjustable deliberation and autonomy, which accounts for cognitive aspects, such as intention revision and belief updates, based on ongoing (runtime) task analysis. This is underpinned by the formal deliberative reasoning logic, extending the more usual Belief-Desire-Intention (BDI) [12] framework, where the Situation Calculus specification is proposed to enable the necessary deliberation and logical deduction to cope with the dynamic nature of the behaviour.

In such circumstances, graphical formalisms, such as Concur Task Tree (CTT) notation, are often utilised for the design and development of user interfaces [13]. A CTT model is comprised of three distinct phases: Firstly tasks are decomposed and arranged into a hierarchical tree-like structure; then temporal relations among tasks are identified; finally objects, associated with each task, and actions, which allow objects to communicate with each other, are identified. The temporal relations allow synchronisation and precedence of tasks allowing the representation of complex temporal dependencies. The CTT notation has been integrated into Teresa [14], a task-based design tool offering facilities for the computer-aided design of User Interfaces. The work described in this paper seeks, additionally, to allow runtime adatation of such models using logical constructs.

The XML-based version of CTT, TERESAXML [15], was the first XML language for task models where logical descriptions of requirements are tranlated into user interface description languages. Similar approaches are followed with XIML [16], UIML [17], and USIXML [18]. These languages, however, are not intended to render the user interface, from the task model, based on user needs or context but rather describe the structure of the interface and the interactions of the interface elements.

UMLi [19] is based on the UML and allows the design and analysis of user interfaces to be achieved through task modelling. Similarly Data Flow Diagrams may be used for the user interface task model, as in Diane+ [20], for example. Further works in modelling user interfaces are available through JUST-UI [21], SUPPLE [22], Teallach [23] and Wisdom [24], whilst model refinement and intention models are used in [25] and [26] respectively. These models capture various features of the user interface requirements based on the given descriptions; generating the user interface automatically based on the task model. Task analysis in these approaches, however, is based on design time user interface models; tasks may become apparrent that are not envisioned within such a preconceived model.

In [2] the notion of plasticity is introduced to cope with multiple contexts for interface deployment: Plasticity is defined as the capacity of an interactive system to maintain usability whilst withstanding variations in the context of use. The work described in this paper seeks such a plasticity of user interface by adapting task models of user interaction to the perceived context through a logical model that is expressed in Situation Calculus. The following Section introduces Situation Calculus whilst demonstrating the benefits of such a treatment.

3 Situation Calculus and Task Modelling

This work takes a logical approach to task modelling for user interface production, necessary to provide cognitive functions for adaptation to context. Recent continuing advances in the representational power of the Situation Calculus language [27] have given a more modular representational style. This has led to applications of the Situation Calculus to many real problems. The original appeal was in applications to cognitive robotics and agent programming [28]. More recently works have appeared addressing the specification and reasoning associated with dynamic and adaptable systems in general such as modelling ubiquitous information services [29] or solving logistics problems with Markov Decision Problems [30]. There are also works progressing on the meta-theory of Situation Calculus improving representational and reasoning techniques. For instance the ramification problem and complex temporal phenomena are addressed in the Inductive Situation Calculus [31].

Informally in Situation Calculus the basic concepts are actions and situations. It provides a quite natural way to represent commonsense type formulations. A situation provides a snapshot of the world that is changed by an action occurrence: Actions are the cause of situation transitions. Each of the situations has a set of fluent values dictated by the initial situation, termed S_0 and the action history. There is a primitive binary operation do; $do(a,s)$ denoting the successor situation to s resulting from performing the action a. Actions are generally denoted by functions and situations (action histories) are first order terms. In seeking to represent a domain actions must have preconditions; necessary conditions that must hold before the action can be performed. The predicate $poss$ is used with $poss(a,s)$ meaning that it is possible to perform the action a in a world resulting from the execution of the sequence of actions s. In order to address the frame problem, effect and frame axioms are combined into one Successor State Axiom [32]. These form the simple, yet highly expressive, primitives of the Situation Calculus. More commonly used formalisms, such as Event Calculus [33], lack the expressive power of the Situation Calculus due to the requirement for a linear time order [34]; counterfactual reasoning is possible in the Situation Calculus yet specifically excluded in the Event Calculus.

The main difference, in using Situation Calculus, from alternative approaches is the concentration on cognition as the driver for system behaviour and observer system function.

3.1 The Situation Calculus Language: Foundational Axioms

More formally the Situation Calculus is a language of three disjoint sorts: Actions or tasks, situations and objects (anything that isn't a task, action or situation, depending on the domain). Generally s and a, with suitable subscripts, will be used for situations and actions respectively. Additionally the language consists of:

- Two function symbols of the sort situation;

    o The constant symbol S_0 denoting the initial situation
    o A binary function $do:action{\times}situation{\rightarrow}situation$. Situations are sequences of actions; $do(a,s)$ is the result of adding the action a to the end of the sequence s.

- A binary predicate symbol $poss:action{\times}situation$: $poss(a,s)$ means it is possible to perform action a in situation s.
- Predicate symbols:

    o Of the sort $(action{\cup}object)^n$ for each $n{\geq}0$ denoting situation independent relations.
    o Of the sort $(action{\cup}object)^n{\times}situation$ for each $n{\geq}0$ denoting relational fluents: Situation dependent relations.

- Function symbols:

  ○   Of the sort $(action \cup object)^n \rightarrow object$ for each $n \geq 0$ denoting situation independent functions.

  ○   Of the sort $(action \cup object)^n \times situation \rightarrow object \cup action$ for each $n \geq 0$ denoting functional fluents: Situation dependent functions.

- Action functions to denote actions of the form $(action \cup object)^n \rightarrow action$ for each $n \geq 0$.

- An ordering relation $\subset situation \times situation$ denoting a subsequence of actions: $s_1 \subset s_2$ means s_1 is a proper subsequence of s_2. Alternatively the situation s_1 occurs before s_2.

The functional and relational fluents take one argument of the sort situation; by convention this is usually the final argument. There are four immediate, domain independent, axioms of the Situation Calculus, which detail the fundamental properties of situations in any domain specific representation of actions and fluents:

1. $do(a_1,s_1) = do(a_2,s_2) \Leftrightarrow (a_1 = a_2) \wedge (s_1 = s_2)$
2. $(\forall P)[P(S_0) \wedge \forall(a,s)\ (P(s) \Rightarrow P(do(a,s)))] \Rightarrow \forall s\ P(s))$
3. $(\neg \exists s)(s \subset S_0)$
4. $s_1 \subset do(a,s_2) \equiv (s_1 \subset s_2) \vee (s_1 = s_2)$

3.2   Task Modelling and Time in Situation Calculus: An Example

In order to show how Situation Calculus may be used for task modeling and the treatment of timing constraints (concurrency, etc.) a generic example is shown here. Actions or tasks occur in time, for certain durations or at the same time as other tasks; it is necessary to consider the ways in which time may be represented within the axioms of the Situation Calculus, as stated up to this point. The formulization described so far only conceives of actions occurring sequentially and without timing constraints. Tasks may occur together and have the same duration; the duration of one may completely envelope the duration of the other or their durations may just overlap. The representational device used within the Situation Calculus to address these problems is to consider instantaneous tasks, which initiate and terminate the task durations with a relational fluent representing the extent of the task. For instance instead of the monolithic task to move some process, A, running at location l_1 to location l_2: $move(A,l_1,l_2)$ the instantaneous tasks *startMove* and *endMove* may be used and the procedure of moving represented by the relational fluent $moving(A,l_1,l_2,s)$: The *startMove* action causing the *moving* fluent to become true with the *endMove* action making it false. Similarly the *communicate* task can be represented by the pair of instantaneous tasks *startCommunicate* and *endCommunicate* with the relational fluent $communicating(s)$. It is then quite simple to represent these actions and fluents in the Situation Calculus, as defined:

$poss(startMove(A,l_1,l_2),s) \Leftrightarrow \neg \exists(l_3,l_4)moving(A, l_3,l_4,s) \wedge location(A,s)=l_1$
$poss(endMove(A,l_1,l_2),s) \Leftrightarrow moving(A, l_1,l_2,s)$

$$moving(A,\ l_1,l_2,do(a,s)) \Leftrightarrow a=startMove(A,l_1,l_2) \lor [\ moving(A,\ l_1,l_2,s) \land$$
$$a \neq endMove(A,l_1,l_2)]$$

$$location(A,do(a,s))=l_2 \Leftrightarrow \exists l_1\ a=endMove(A,l_1,l_2) \lor [\ location(A,s)=l_2 \land$$
$$\neg(\exists l,l')\ a \neq endMove(A,l,l')]$$

With this representation complex concurrency can be handled. For example for a particular process:

{startMove(l_1,l_2), startBroadcast},{endBroadcast, startReplication(l_3)}, {endMove(l_1,l_2)}

is the sequence of tasks commencing with simultaneously starting to move from l_1 to l_2 and broadcast, followed by simultaneously ending the broadcast and starting to replicate at location l_3, followed by ending the move at l_2 whilst the replication is still proceeding.

This gives a particularly concise representation for interleaved concurrency: Two tasks are interleaved if one is the next action to occur after the other. Thus an interleaved concurrent representation can be given for moving and broadcasting, for instance:

do([startMove(l_1,l_2),startBroadcast,endBroadcast, endMove(l_1,l_2)],S_0)

where broadcasting is initiated after a move is started and terminated before the end of the move. Alternatively it might be the case that:

do([startBroadcast, startMove(l_1,l_2), endBroadcast, endMove(l_1,l_2)],S_0)

Thus any overlapping occurrences of moving and broadcasting, except for exact co-occurrences of the initiating or terminating actions, may be realised in the formalism. This is achieved without having to extend the formalism in any way.

To incorporate time into the Situation Calculus does involve extending the foundational axioms with one new axiom and introducing two new functions. The representational device for denoting time, in the Situation Calculus, is simply to add a temporal argument to actions. Thus *startBroadcast(t)* is the instantaneous action of the broadcast starting at time t. The first new function is devoted to extracting this time argument from the representation: It is a function *time:actions*→ $\Re$.*time(a)* where $\Re$ is the set of real numbers. So, for example *time(startBroadcast(t))=t*. The second new function is *start:situation*→ $\Re$. *start(s)*, which denotes the start time of situation s. This gives rise to the new foundational axiom, which may be succinctly stated as; *start(do(a,s))=time(a)*. This facility to express time allows for the representation of any complex interleaving processes. In Figure 1 the time line is illustrated where there are three overlapping processes: The movement of a process (say) from location x to location y (*moving(x,y,s)*); the replication of the process at location x (*replicating(x,s)*) and the communication with another process A (*communicating(A,s)*). The *moving* and *replicating* procedures begin together at t=0 with the *replicating* finishing at t=3 and the *moving* at t=4. The *communicating* procedure is already occurring in the initial situation (t=0) and finishes at the same time as the *moving* procedure (t=4).

Finally, in dealing with modelling temporal aspects of dynamic systems, it is possible to handle true concurrency; when one or more actions happen at the same time. This is achieved by simply considering concurrent actions as sets of simple actions:

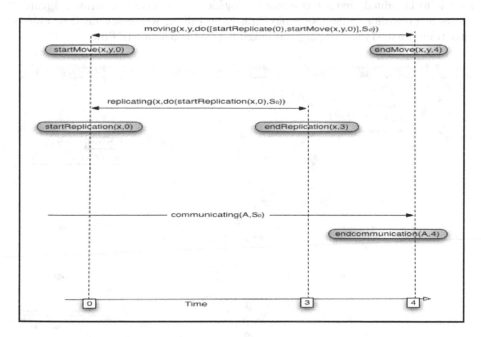

Fig. 1. Interleaved time processes for tasks in situation calculus

The notation $a \in A$ denotes that the simple task action a is one of the tasks of the concurrent action A. The *do* function symbol can be extended to accept concurrent actions as arguments: $do(\{startMove(x,y),openFile(f)\},S_0)$, for example. The foundational axioms, as previously stated, are then composed exactly as for simple actions; a concurrent action set replaces the simple action in the axioms. The action precondition axioms then become: endMove

$$poss(a,s) \Rightarrow poss(\{a\},s) \text{ and}$$
$$poss(A,s) \Rightarrow (\exists a)a \in A \wedge (\forall a)[a \in A \Rightarrow poss(a,s)]$$

The successor state axioms can also be adapted to take account of concurrent actions, for instance:

$$moving(x,y,do(A,s)) \Leftrightarrow startMove(x,y) \in A \vee moving(x,y,s) \wedge endMove(x,y) \notin A$$

4   A Task Analysis Flow Editor

To model and verify the task analysis from the Situation Calculus representation, in a visual setting, a task flow editor has been developed. This is based in the Neptune language [35], a custom made scripting language, which implements a version of the

Situation Calculus successor state axioms. Any full description of Neptune is outside the scope of this paper but further details can be found in the references. The Neptune IDE (Integrated Development Environment) uses a graphical interface to allow flow models to be edited, and a text editor for logical statements to be written. Figure 2 shows a screenshot of the (Neptune) Task Flow Editor, where several flow objects have been dropped onto the page and linked to provide a notion of flow.

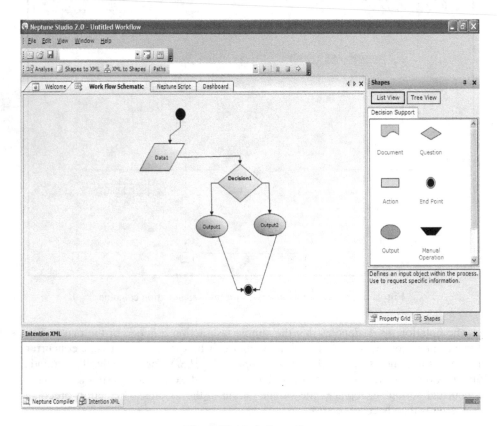

Fig. 2. The task flow editor

A more complete description of the architecture can be found in [36]. Briefly stated, Neptune provides an implementation of the Situation Calculus formal task model: Sucessor state axioms are encoded to provide the predicted outcomes of actions for the model and meta-model. Tools exist that allow step-by-step walkthroughs of the possible routes available through the model, so that errors in logic, such as flows that repeat and loop indefinitely, can be identified and rectified accordingly. In summary, by dropping these shapes onto the diagram, linking them, and encoding the logic behind the model, a complete decision process task model can be created and adapted externally from a software system. The software then executes this model, and behaves according to the model and associated meta-model giving an initial task model that is refined and adapted as the system evolves.The paths through the model are analyzed and verified on compilation: The result for Figure 2 is shown in Figure 3.

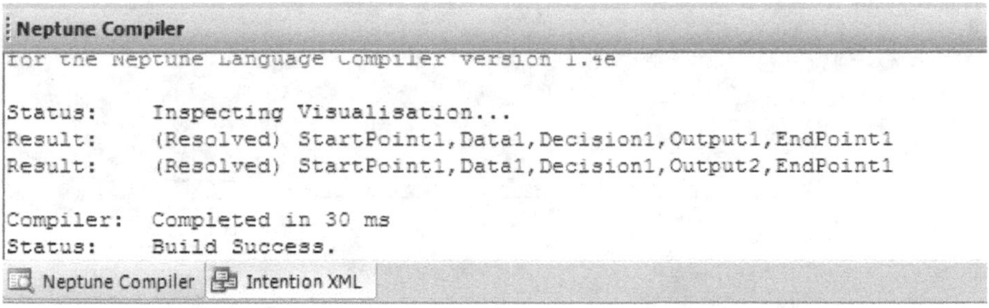

Fig. 3. Flow Editor Output

5 Case Study

It can be seen from the preceding sections how task analysis may be modelled, in the Situation Calculus and visually checked, through the flow editor. The following section outlines how the techniques were used to produce an adaptable, distributed guideline model for a breast-cancer decision support system [37]. In this project, one goal of the system was that it should adapt its classification of patient treatment based on historical evidence to improve the level of care given to patients. A guideline decision process published by National Institute of Clinical Excellence (NICE), UK [38] was subjected to task analysis in the Situation Calculus and was used as a base upon which to decide on treatment for a patient.

Theoretical management requirements were introduced so that certain treatments were no longer available and that given a choice between treatments, the cheaper would be preferable. While the NICE guidelines remained static, these new requirements were added, as new decisions, to supplement the original model, thereby adapting its behaviour. Figure 4 shows part of a typical task flow model validated by the Neptune IDE task flow editor.

In addition, as the Situation Calculus task and meta-task models provide a formal model for the tasks involved, when a patient profile is executed against the NICE guidelines, comprehensive historical data is generated, which can later form the basis of evidence given to machine-learning and data-mining processes. This study of usage enabled deviations from guidelines by clinicians to be audited and presented accordingly. Another consequence of having a flexible task model for charting patients progress through the decision model was that patients modelled in the prototype could return to the hospital at a later date and clinicians would be presented with both the patient details and the exact reasoning behind the decisions of the information system, essential in ascertaining correct patient care. A clinician using this system has a profile of acceptable behaviour, and a preferential functionality profile. Thus, the clinician when using the system from any access point will be granted access to the resources required; enabling acceptable behaviour; in essence, the Quality of Process (QoP) concerns to be fulfilled. For example, if the clinician uses a particular task model, and often applies a range of "What-If" questions upon the model, the system will adapt the model to the clinician's concerns: Thus, when a clinician logs into the system their local decision model is obtained from the task model with its specialisations applied.

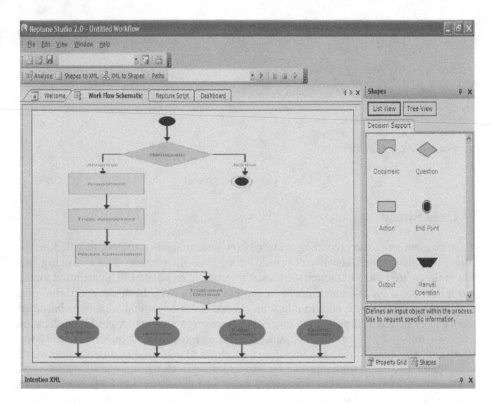

Fig. 4. Typical treatment task flow

As validation, the predicted state holds when the local decision model copy equates to the remote decision model (such evaluation is determined by checking the unique IDs of both models, as they should be the same). For example, clinicians using the system from a hospital other than their own could be exposed to the local task models of that hospital, as well as the models used by their own hospital. Thus, based on the environmental information, the execution state can be influenced. For example the decision support system considered in this case study was required to output tasks and treatment options based on rule sets with patient data as inputs. Additionally, the system was also required to exhibit adaptation of task to context. Thus, for instance, a simple treatment rule for using the drug tamoxifen, which is recommended in the guidelines for post menopausal patients with positive oestrogen receptors, can be formally stated as:

$NICEtreatment(patient,tamoxifen,do(a,s)) \Leftrightarrow [NICEtreatment(patient,tamoxifen,s) \wedge$
$\neg \exists treatment(a=nice\_treament\_decision(patient, treatment) \wedge$
$(treatment \neq tamoxifen))] \vee [a=nice\_treatment\_decision(patient,tamoxifen)]$
   with
$poss(nice\_treatment\_decision(patient,tamoxifen),s) \Rightarrow (oesreceptor(patient,s)=pos) \wedge$
$(menostatus(patient,s)=post)$

Similar rules can, trivially, be stated for the other options, within NICE or any other set of guidelines. The rules governing the task adaptation meta-system are required to reason over the operation of the system. A quality of process concern may involve assessing the clinician's adherence to a specified guideline treatment:

$$compliance(patient, treatment, service\_decision, do(a, s)) \Leftrightarrow$$
$$[compliance(patient, treatment, service\_decision, s) \land$$
$$a \neq treament\_decision(patient, treatment1)] \lor$$
$$[a = treatment\_decision(patient, treatment) \land$$
$$service\text{-}decision(patient, s) = treatment]$$

In order to express the efficacy of the treatment decisions for the quality of process it is appropriate to consider the outcomes of courses of treatment, which occur over a period of time. It is thus necessary to employ the Situation Calculus technique that deals with the duration of actions. Therefore the treatment duration is covered by two instantaneous actions *startTreatment* and *endTreatment* with a fluent *treating* through the duration of the treatment. So, for a patient *p*, continuing with the example of tamoxifen treatment given above, there may be a reward function such as:

$$reward(treatment(p, tamoxifen), do(a, s)) = r \Leftrightarrow a = endTreatment(p, tamoxifen) \land$$

$$(r = 100 \land living(p, s)) \lor (r = -500 \land \neg living(p, s))]$$

with

$$fitness((treatment(tamoxifen) \land menostatus(p, s) = post \land oesreceptor(p, s) = pos), do(a, s)) =$$

$$fitness((treatment(tamoxifen) \land menostatus(p, s) = post \land oesreceptor(p, s) = pos), s) +$$

$$reward(treatment(p, tamoxifen), do(a, s))$$

In this way the success of each rule occurrence can be assessed including previously untried treatments instigated by the clinician and flagged for non-compliance. Thus less successful treatments will be deleted from the decision options whilst the decisions that lead to more favourable results will be chosen and integrated into the task flow model, improving the quality of the process.

6 Conclusions and Future Work

This work is concerned with a task driven model of computational environments and proposes the formal setting of Situation Calculus as a flexible and useful notation for task modelling. In addition the Neptune IDE task flow editor has been developed to take as input the formally stated task model and meta-model, checking consistency, and output the code for the meta-model allowing variation and adaptation of the task model to observed circumstance. Additionally the task flow editor may also be used to output the formal model from a user generated task flow. In establishing a task model and an observer based meta-model in the Situation Calculus it is possible to specify reasoning and deliberation on the tasks through the logic, without an exhaustive enumeration of the entire state space.

Predominant in this approach is the handling of temporal aspects within the Situation Calculus, both relatively, in terms of ordering, and absolutely for timed events: In relation to the requirements, of task modelling and the automatic runtime maintenance and tuning of large-scale, complex, distributed task models, the major weak point of most approaches is the necessary enumeration of all possible states in advance. Such enumeration is impossible for this work as the evolution of large-scale complex systems is, in general, not predictable [39]. Even if enumeration were possible changes in state compositions would result in an exponential increase in the number of system states. Furthermore any practical utilisation, including the facility for deliberation on the system by itself, requires the additional provision of modelling and verification methods to sit above the primitive constructs of the formalism [40]. Thus the need for a formalism giving a "propositional account" has been established. This naturally leads to the adoption of mathematical logic: Instead of enumerating states and their transition functions, a sentence describing what is true in the system and its environment and the causal laws in effect for that environment are favoured. This means that: task models are determined by the logical consequences of the systems description, through entailment; a non-procedural specification is provided where properties may be verified and logical deduction used to establish correctness of the task flow and a task model specification is obtained that is executable, giving a formal system simulator. Throughout this work the formalism used is required not only to model the systems' tasks but also to provide the deliberative functions for met-task analysis.

The task flow editor in the Neptune IDE represents the direction of future work in this area: It is envisaged that an automated process will enable the generation of a fully coded user interface, in line with the current system circumstances, from the formal task flow model and observation specfied in the Situation Calculus language.

References

1. Zhenyu, W., Garlan, D.: Task-driven computing, Technical Report, NO. CMU-CS-00-154. Carnegie Mellon University (May 2000),
   http://www-2.cs.cmu.edu/~aura/docdir/wang00.pdf
2. Thevenin, D., Coutaz, J.: Adaptivity and Plasticity of User Interfaces. In: 7th IFIP Conference on Human-Computer Interaction, Edinburgh, Scotland, pp. 110–117 (1999)
3. Randles, M., Taleb-Bendiab, A., Miseldine, P.: Addressing the Signal Grounding Problem for Autonomic Systems. In: Proceedings of International Conference on Autonomic and Autonomous Systems (ICAS 2006), Santa Clara, USA, July 19-21, p. 21 (2006)
4. Levesque, H.J., Pirri, F., Reiter, R.: Foundations for the Situation Calculus. Linköping Electronic Articles in Computer and Information Science (1998),
   http://www.ep.liu.se/ea/cis/1998/018/
5. McCarthy, J., Hayes, P.: Some Philosophical Problems from the Standpoint of Artificial Intelligence. Machine Intelligence 4(1), 463–502 (1968)
6. Dey, A.: Providing Architectural Support for Building Context-Aware Applications. PhD Thesis. College of Computing, Georgia Institute of Technology, USA, 170 p. (2000)
7. Ni, H., Zhou, X., Yu, Z., Miao, K.: OWL-Based Context-Dependent Task Modeling and Deducing. In: Proceeding of the 21st International conference on Advanced Information Networking and Applications Workshops (AINAW 2007), pp. 846–851 (2007)

8. Castro, P., Muntz, R.: Managing Context Data for Smart Spaces. IEEE Personal Communications 7, 44–46 (2000)
9. Prekop, P., Burnett, M.: Activities, Context and Ubiquitous Computing. Computer Communications 26(11), 1168–1176 (2003)
10. Taleb-Bendiab, A., England, D., Randles, M., Miseldine, P., Murphy, K.: A Principled Approach to the Design of Healthcare Systems: Autonomy vs. Governance. Reliability Engineering & System Safety 91(12), 1576–1585 (2006); Complexity in Design and Engineering
11. Bailey, J., Poulovassilis, A., Wood, P.T.: An Event-Condition-Action Language for XML. In: WWW 2002, Honolulu, Hawaii, USA, pp. 7–11 (2001)
12. Bratman, M.E.: Intentions, plans and practical reason. Harvard University Press, Cambridge (1987)
13. Paternò, F., Mancini, C., Meniconi, S.: ConcurTaskTrees: A Diagrammatic Notation for Specifying Task Models. In: Proceedings of the IFIP TC13 International Conference on Human-Computer Interaction (INTERACT 1997), pp. 362–369. Chapman & Hall, Boca Raton (1997)
14. Paternò, F., Santoro, C.: One Model, Many Interfaces. In: Proceedings of CADUI 2002, pp. 143–154. Kluwer Academics, Dordrecht (2002)
15. Mori, G., Paterno, F., Santoro, C.: Design and Development of Multidevice User Interfaces through Multiple Logical Descriptions. IEEE Transactions on Software Engineering 8, 1–14 (2004)
16. Puerta, A., Eisenstein, J.: XIML: A Common Representation for Interaction Data. In: 7th International Conference on Intelligent User Interfaces, pp. 214–215 (2002)
17. Mir Farooq, A., Abrams, M.: Simplifying Construction of Multi-Platform User Interfaces using UIML. In: European Conference UIML (2001)
18. Limbourg, Q., Vanderdonckt, J.: UsiXML: A User Interface Description Language Supporting Multiple Levels of Independence. In: Engineering Advanced Web Applications (2004)
19. da Silva, P.P., Paton, N.W.: User Interface Modeling inUMLi. IEEE Software 20(4), 62–69 (2003)
20. Tarby, J., Barthet, M.: The DIANE+ Method. In: Computer-Aided Design of User Interfaces, pp. 95–119. Namur University Press, Namur (1996)
21. Molina, P.J., Meliá, S., Pastor, O.: JUST-UI: A User Interface Specification Model. In: Proceedings of CADUI, pp. 63–74 (2002)
22. Gajos, K., Weld, D.S.: SUPPLE: Automatically Generating User Interfaces. In: Proceedings of IUI, pp. 83–100 (2004)
23. Griffiths, T., Barclay, P.: Teallach: A model-based user interface development environment for object databases. Interacting with Computers 1, 31–68 (2001)
24. Jardim Nunes, N., Falcão e Cunha, J.: Wisdom - A UML based architecture for interactive systems. In: Palanque, P., Paternó, F. (eds.) DSV-IS 2000. LNCS, vol. 1946, pp. 191–205. Springer, Heidelberg (2001)
25. Bowen, J., Reeves, S.: Formal refinement of informal GUI design artefacts. In: Software Engineering Conference, pp. 221–230 (2006)
26. Bisignano, M., Di Modica, G., Tomarchio, O.: An'intent-oriented' approach for Multi-Device User Interface Design. In: 20th International Conference on Advanced Information Networking and Applications, pp. 186–194 (2006)
27. Kelly, R.F., Pearce, A.R.: Property Persistence in the Situation Calculus. In: Proc. of the International Joint Conference on Artificial Intelligence (IJCAI 2007), pp. 1948–1953 (2007)

28. Lesperance, Y., Levesque, H., Reiter, R.: A Situation Calculus Approach to Modeling and Programming Agents. In: Rao, A., Wooldridge, M. (eds.) Foundations and Theories of Rational Agency. Kluwer Academic Press, New York (1997)
29. Dong, W., Xu, K., Lin, M.: A Situation Calculus-based Approach To Model Ubiquitous Information Services. Computing Research Repository (CoRR) cs.AI/0311052 (2004), http://arxiv.org/abs/cs.AI/0311052 (last accessed May 2009)
30. Sanner, S., Boutilier, C.: Practical Linear Value-approximation Techniques for First-order MDPs. In: Proceedings of the 22nd Conference on Uncertainty in Artificial Intelligence. AUAI Press, Arlington (2006)
31. Denecker, M., Ternovska, E.: Inductive Situation Calculus. Artificial Intelligence 171 (5-6), 332–360 (2007)
32. Reiter, R.: Knowledge in Action. MIT Press, Cambridge (2001)
33. Kowalski, R.A., Sergot, M.: A Logic Based Calculus of Events. New Generation Computing 4(4), 319–340 (1986)
34. van Belleghem, K., Denecker, M., De Schreye, D.: On the Relation between Situation Calculus and Event Calculus. The Journal of Logic Programming 31(1-3), 3–37 (1997)
35. Miseldine, P., Taleb-Bendiab, A.: A Programmatic Approach to Applying Sympathetic and Parasympathetic Autonomic Systems to Software Design. In: Czap, H., et al. (eds.) Self-Organisation and Autonomic Informatics (1), pp. 293–303. IOS Press, Amsterdam (2005)
36. Miseldine, P., Taleb-Bendiab, A., England, D., Randles, M.: Addressing the need for adaptable decision processes within healthcare software. Informatics for Health and Social Care 32(1), 35–41 (2007)
37. The 2nrich Project, http://www.cms.livjm.ac.uk/2nrich
38. NICE, National Institute for Clinical Excellence (2009), http://www.nice.org.uk
39. Bullock, S., Cliff, D.: Complexity and Emergent Behaviour in ICT Systems. Technical Report HP-2004-187, Semantic & Adaptive Systems, Hewlett-Packard Labs (2004), http://www.hpl.hp.com/techreports/2004/HPL-2004-187.pdf
40. Cerone, A., Milne, G.J.: Property Verification of Asynchronous Systems. Innovations in Systems and Software Engineering 1(1), 25–40 (2005)

Formally Expressing the Users' Objects World in Task Models

Sybille Caffiau[1,2], Patrick Girard[1], Dominique L. Scapin[2], Laurent Guittet[1], and Loé Sanou[1]

[1] Laboratoire d'Informatique Scientifique et Industrielle, Téléport 2-1 avenue Clément Ader, 86961 Futuroscope Cedex, France
{sybille.caffiau,girard,guittet,sanou}@ensma.fr
[2] Institut National de Recherche en Informatique et en Automatique, Domaine de Voluceau -Rocquencourt- B.P.105, 78153, Le Chesnay, France
Dominique.Scapin@inria.fr

Abstract. While past research presents objects as essential entities in task modeling, they are in fact rarely used. In the first tool that truly considered objects, K-MADe, two main reasons may explain this limited use: an incomplete module of object description (in the tool, the expression coverage of the object concept is not wide enough) and the usability problems of K-MADe's specific interface. This paper presents a study on the object expression coverage. From case studies, we identify limitations and we infer modification on the K-MADe object entity definitions. These modifications aim to increase the expressive power of objects.

Keywords: Task models, Objects, User-centered Design, K-MADe.

1 Introduction

The first step in the design of interactive applications is the specification definition. In user-centered approaches, this specification step takes into account the user requirements. In order to express the collection of the user requirements, models -named task models- have been developed [1, 2]. Task models are composed of several entities. These entities aim, in a more or less formal way, to describe the user activities. As task models may support the design of applications adapted to carry out the activities described in such models, this description ought to be closer to what user's reality is. Sinning et al. proposed in [3] a study of the extensions that can increase the CTT task models [4] expression to interactive application design. These extensions concern the operator set, the structural enhancements of task models (how to express the task model structure) and the specific needs of cooperative task models. The CTT notation does not formally integrate handled objects that are described as essential to describe activities in its whole [5-8]. Then, the proposed extensions do not take into account the expression power of objects. However, previous studies showed benefits of the present of object for task model designers [6, 8, 9]. Our goal is to go further in the study of the limitations of task models by considering object management under the

D. England et al. (Eds.): TAMODIA 2009, LNCS 5963, pp. 117–130, 2010.

point of view of the design expression. These studies are empirical assessments of K-MADe usage when learning [10] and designing [9] task modeling. They show that while the use of objects in task models is intuitive for designers, their usage still remains difficult.

From the results of a previous study performed on task model expressive extensions [3], we focused our study on extensions due to limitations on scheduling (operator set extensions). Furthermore, we identified other extensions less object-dependant, presented in sections 5 and 6. In order to conduct this study, we used K-MADe [11], the most expressive tool in term of object. In the next section, we present the comparison of the five task model tools that integrate handled objects (CTTE [4], Euterpe [8], IMAD [12, 13], K-MADe [11, 14] and AMBOSS [15]), and the previous studies on K-MADe objects. We conducted a case study evaluation, in order to investigate the limitations of the expression power of task model that include objects. These case studies are performed by students or designer experts in several contexts, each designer indicating K-MADe limitations and difficulties (in reports or interviews) during the designs or at the end of the modeling. From these case study designs, we detected some object expression limitations and attended to give rationale for such limitations. Finally, we propose some object definition modifications in order to improve the description of an activity.

This study aims to: identify the current limitations of the object expression to design task models that will support user-centered design; and propose modifications to increase the expressive power of objects. The presented limitations are identified from the task model design of several activities that will be described in the third section. The results of this study are classified into three sections. The first one presents the limitations and modifications for the K-MADe object use in order to express requirements for design. The next two sections present results on the definition of object modules: attributes and groups.

2 Background and Related Work

In task models, objects characterize the environment of the user. They are icons or concepts the user handles or that influence the course of his/her activity. Five task model tools currently integrate objects in their models: CTTE [4], Euterpe [8], IMAD [12, 13], K-MADe [11, 14] and AMBOSS [15]. First, we compare the expression power of objects in these five tools in order to justify our choice to base the object study on K-MADe objects. We then, shortly summarize previous studies focused on K-MADe objects.

2.1 Objects in Task Model Tools

The five tools that integrate objects in their implemented model do not identically consider and define such objects (Table 1). According to the considered object, they can be divided into two categories. First, the tools considering objects as task attributes (such as CTTE), and secondly the tools considering objects as first class components (such as Euterpe, IMAD, K-MADe and AMBOSS). The definition of objects as task attributes requires that objects are transferred to other tasks by using operators in order to perform several tasks.

Table 1. Expression Power of Objects in Task Model Tools

Tools	CTTE	Euterpe	IMAD	K-MADe	AMBOSS
Abstract object	-	-	√	√	√
Concrete object	√	√	√	√	-
Attribute name	not formally	√	√	√	√
Attribute type	not formally	-	√	√	not formally
Attribute value	*not formally*	√	-	√	-
Use	√	-	-	√	-

Moreover, two kinds of objects are present in these tools: *abstract objects* (objects without any value) and *concrete objects* (object instances). While objects defined in CTTE and Euterpe are concrete (a value is associated to the object), IMAD and AMBOSS do not allow to set a value to object attributes. Thus, these two tools remain at an abstract level of definition. This level of definition freezes the manipulation of task model objects (in a dynamic way), which limits the expression to a static state of the world representation.

The two object categories (abstract and concrete) are only both defined in K-MADe, and represent two definition levels:

- abstract level: characteristics related to the concept handled by the user with abstract attributes (characteristics of the abstract object)
- concrete level: correspond to an instance of an abstract object with concrete attributes (that allows to assign a value for each characteristic of the abstract attributes of the abstract objects).

For example, an email from an abstract definition level is an object with a date, one (or several) addressee address(es), a subject, a message... and from a concrete definition level, it is the email that is sent today, to the supervisor...

In addition, while Euterpe, IMAD and AMBOSS objects contribute only to describe the environment of the user, the CTTE and K-MADe objects are used in several design steps.

In CTTE, a particular object attribute is its cardinality. It is used to help the designer to define the interactive element that represents that object [16]. Moreover, perceivable objects may be a table or a window and thus, this tool associates interactive objects to tasks. The introduction of these elements (cardinalities and perceivable objects) in the task model formalism illustrates the link between handled objects and interface presentation. This definition is close to a system-based point of view whereas in all other tools, object concepts try to focus on ergonomics aspects.

In K-MADe, objects are used in order to express formal conditions (as task pre-conditions). All the formalisms include the pre-conditions associated to the tasks. While CTTE, Euterpe and IMAD expressed these pre-conditions as strings, AMBOSS expressed pre-conditions as a necessary presence of barriers and messages. However, both elements are expressed as strings themselves. In order to specify the consequences of a task execution on the handled objects, Euterpe, IMAD and K-MADe include post-condition expressions. The Euterpe and IMAD post-conditions are therefore expressed as strings without any link with objects and without any possibility to take the object values into account. K-MAD is the only formalism that allows to define formal expressions with objects. In K-MADe, objects are defined by a *name* (labels 1 in Figure 1) and *attributes* (in boxes in Figure 1). Abstract objects are composed of *abstract attributes* (attribute name and *value type* (label 2 in Figure 1)) and concrete objects are composed of concrete attributes (*value* according to the abstract attribute type (label 3 in Figure 1)). Concrete objects are organized into *groups* (label 4 in Figure 1), which are defined by a *name* and an aggregation *type* from list, stack, set and singleton. Figure 2 from [11] shows the relationship between abstract objects, concrete objects and groups.

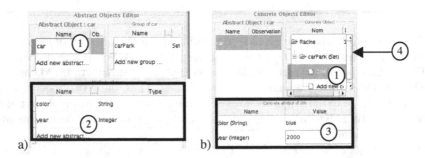

Fig. 1. K-MADe a) abstract object editor and b) concrete object editor

Validations of the conditions are mandatory for task execution. Therefore, these conditions need to be computed to allow the validation of task models by the user and consequently the verification of the task scheduling (using simulation). In order to compute the conditions, the definitions of used entities and conditions have to be formalized. Using defined objects to express these conditions allows to formally take into account the environment of the user to complete the scheduling [9] and to have a dynamic model (due to the association between task and the potential side effects via post-conditions). In order to benefit from these formal definitions, task model object expressive power has to be the widest possible.

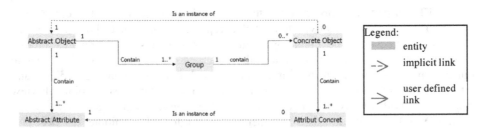

Fig. 2. Relations between abstract objects, concrete objects and groups (from the K-MADe user manual)

By using calculators (in the K-MADe tool), task model designers can defined formal conditions (Figure 3a) and side effects that will be computed when scenarios will be performed (Figure 3b).

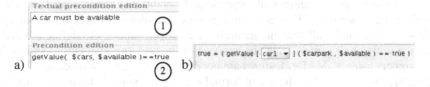

Fig. 3. a) An edited formal pre-condition and b) a computed result (task can be performed)

2.2 Previous Work on K-MADe Objects

Due to their formal description, previous empirical evaluations focused on K-MADe objects. These assessments aimed at evaluating the apprenticeship [10] and the use of objects [9]. They provided results that may be classified in two main points: results about the definition of formal objects and results about their use.

K-MADe formal objects are mainly defined after the task decomposition, to add complementary information. We observed that the formal entities are defined in order to add semantics to the K-MADe tasks. For an actor, the task definition is not disconnected from the definition of entities that are manipulated to perform the task. For example, to describe a communication by email, users specify the handled objects ("Then, I send the email") (Figure 4). However, the definition of tasks without any object limits the semantics to the task name and, is therefore dependant of the task model reading. On the contrary, the association of objects (used in the conditions) formally describes the task behavior (execution conditions and effects). Thus, the addition of objects associated to the tasks improves the understanding and consequently, the communication between all the application design actors (one of the six evaluation in [1]).

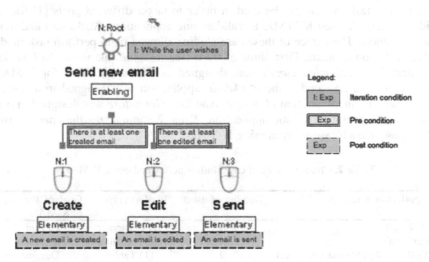

Fig. 4. Graphical representation of a short task model with textual representation of its preconditions (green), post-conditions (blue) and iteration (purple)

In addition to this semantic goal, objects (and conditions) are also used in order to complete the scheduling. This contribution appears quickly to task model designer students (for example, all students naturally used formal entities to define the ending state of a volley-ball game). Thus, the analysis of the previous evaluations shows that, for designers using K-MADe, features are necessary to design task models.

Finally, the main goal of the use of formal entities is to enable their computation in order to perform validation. As the empirical evaluation shows, the most used entities are the ones that can be computed and used in the K-MADe verification tools. However, the K-MADe evaluations also indicated that designers often define informal conditions (in textual description (label 1 in Figure 3a)) when they do not succeed at defining the formal definition (label 2 in Figure 3a).

Thus, while these assessment results show that object concepts seem to be essential in the task model process (which supports past research that suggested the need to introduce objects [7, 8]), they also pointed out difficulties of use. Two main reasons may explain these difficulties: limitation on the expressive power of objects in the implemented kernel of K-MAD; and the interactive limitations in the tool. In order to determine the impact of the first issue, we conducted a study of the K-MADe coverage power by designing several case studies.

3 Case Studies

In order to study the real coverage power of K-MADe objects, we used K-MADe to model five different activities. The case studies were chosen to study the modeling of the widest characteristics of the interactive applications. Then, we designed application task models corresponding to activities with different user group sizes, types of system, and platforms.

Moreover, task models can be used in order to target different goals [1] (design, validation,...). We used K-MADe to validate one application (*ParAdmin*) and to design four others. The choice of these case studies allowed us to perform task models in three different contexts. First, three of them (the *webmail*, the *volley ball marking sheet* and the *Mastermind game*) were designed as first applications for K-MADe usability purposes. Secondly, the *ParAdmin* application was designed in a research context, with frequent iteration of design. And last, *Genindexe* was designed in order to produce an operational static application. Table 2 summarizes the characteristics and purpose of each case study in using K-MAD.

Table 2. Characteristics of case studies performed using K-MADe

Application reference	Number of users	Platform type	Goal of the use of K-MAD
Webmail	1	(1) Computer	Design
ParAdmin	1	(1) Computer	Validation
Volley-ball game marking sheet	1	(1) Tablet	Design
Mastermind	1 or 2	(1) Computer	Design
Genindexe	All employees	(4) Computer	Design

Webmail. The first application is a classic webmail application. This design is based on a task model expressing all activities that allow communication by email (address book management, email production, management of received emails,...). This case study was designed by two users (a novice and an expert).

ParAdmin. In order to study the role of the K-MADe task model to validate an application interface, we modeled the management of a data warehouse. A tool, named *ParAdmin* [17], was developed in a first version, without any task analysis, an for use by the developer only. In order to allow its use by a larger group of people, a task model analysis was performed with K-MADe. An HCI expert and the *ParAdmin* developer jointly designed the task model of this case study.

Volley ball game marking sheet. The last single user activity is the completion of a volley ball game marking sheet (during a game). This activity is traditionally performed using a paper sheet. The goal of the design of this activity is to migrate to a tablet platform and then, to automate calculations and verifications (for example, to evaluate from the data entered whether a game is finished or not). This case study was used in an object use assessment unit [9]. It was designed by 68 students.

Mastermind. The design of the mastermind game shows the needs of an application used simultaneously by several users. This game was developed to be used on computers by one or two people. Several task models were designed, corresponding to the several versions of the application game. Two users (a novice and an expert, the same as for the *Webmail* task model) designed these task models.

Genindexe. The last application was designed for managing the activity of an biological analysis laboratory. A task model is designed to create an application adapted to the activities of all employees according to their security requirements. 48 students (postgraduates, at the end of their learning unit on task model analysis) designed the task model of this activity.

From the design of these task models we observed some expressive limitations that we present in the next sections.

4 Object Use to Increase Task Model Expressivity

In a previous study on task model extensions [3], a proposition of new operators were made. This study proposed the addition of several operators: the *stop* operator (to specify the unsuccessful termination of a task), the *deterministic* and *non-deterministic choice* operators and the *instance iteration* operator (to express the iteration of several instances). K-MAD was not defined in order to express unsuccessful tasks thus, the *stop* operator (operator proposed in [3] to express the unsuccessful termination of a task) is not in the K-MAD model. Moreover, the deterministic choice is expressed in K-MADe by using object expressions. K-MADe objects can be computed in three expressions of condition: the *pre-condition* (conditions for the task to be achievable), the called *post-condition* (actions resulting from the task, i.e. dynamics of the model objects: modification of the attribute values, creation or removal of objects) and the *iteration condition* (conditions for the task repetition). To edit the computable expressions, designers use condition calculators (Figure 5). They are composed of several parts.

Two of these parts represent the operation definition: the *operator* part and the *function* part. They illustrate all the operations available on objects. First, we outline the limitation of the operator coverage. Second, we focus our analysis on the specific needs of the iteration condition expression.

4.1 Operators

One of the calculator parts presents the set of mathematical operators (lFigure 5). The study of data description model (in UML/OCL [18] and EXPRESS [19]) determines the necessity of thirteen mathematical operators: three logical operators (AND, OR, NOT); four arithmetic operators (+, -, *, /); and six relationship operators (=, <, >, !=, >=, <=).

All the logical operators and relationship operators exists in K-MADe. The post-condition calculator possesses two arithmetic operations: the addition and the subtraction. In addition to these arithmetic operations, the multiplication and the division operations have to be added.

Fig. 5. Pre-condition and post-condition calculators

4.2 Iteration Expressions

In K-MADe, task iteration is set up by an expression. This expression may be defined by a number (fixed number of task repetitions) or a Boolean expression (task is repeated while the condition is true). These iteration expressions do not cover all the iterations that designers have to express. Some iterations are not defined by computable expressions but by the user initiative. For example, a user adds email addressees whenever and as much as s/he whishes. In order to represent this specific condition, an iteration condition expression that collects the user whishes (to repeat or stop) can be defined. However, the end of a task iteration process by a user is semantically different from an end due to the modification of the objects state. Thus, we prefer to split the iteration control into two different types: a model-controlled iteration type and an actor-controlled iteration type. In CTT, only one iteration type is defined, a non-controlled iteration (*). An iterative task ends when the next one interrupts it. The study presented in [3] does not detected the limitations due to this uncontrolled iteration.

However, it illustrates another limitation that the designer cannot express tasks on several instances of an object (*instance iteration* in [3]) at the same time, for example, the concurrent edition of several emails. Sinning et al. proposes to add another scheduling characteristic that specifies this particular iteration. Thus, two different kinds of iteration will specify the task iteration characteristics: first, the sequential task iteration (task executions are sequentially performed) and secondly, the instance task iteration (iteration of instances). This feature allows the distinction of the two different iteration concepts.

Therefore, K-MADe will allow three different iteration types: (1) the *instance* task iteration, (2) the model-controlled iteration and (3) the actor-controlled iteration (with (2) and (3) the controlled iterations).

5 Definition of Object Attributes

In order to define K-MAD objects, their attributes are defined. These attributes are composed of their name and their type. The type defines the domain of the attribute value. The available types in K-MADe are: *Integer, Boolean* and *String*.

The use of K-MADe in order to design several task models highlights some limitations due to the available types. We split this set of issues into two groups according to the levels of type definition: the simple and constructed attribute types. The *simple attribute* types are attribute types that are not composed. In K-MADe, all the current defined attribute types are simple. However, the set of the available simple types does not cover all the attribute values that the designer wants to describe. In addition to these simple attributes, constructed attributes are mandatory in order to complete the object definition.

5.1 Simple Attribute Types

While no limitation on textual attribute (String) and binary attribute (Boolean) definitions are raised, the coverage of the numeric attribute (Integer) does not take into account all the potential numeric values. For example, from the set of objects used to express the amount conversion, a defined object is the amount (that will be converted). The type of this value being a number, we expressed it using an integer. However, this definition limits the set of values used and computable (by using a simulation tool for example).

In order to express numeric values, EXPRESS [19] and UML/OCL [18] (two other data expression languages) possess several numeric types (real, float, integer). Regarding the wide possibility of the definition type for both languages, we propose to increase the expressivity power of the object attributes by adding the *float* type to the *integer* type.

Both languages (UML/OCL and EXPRESS) are used by computer specialists who know the type names as integer or real. On the contrary, K-MADe users may be non-experts in computer science. We consider the cost of apprenticeship of the numeric type differences too important for the provided benefits. Thus, we propose to change the *Integer* type into the *Numeric* type. This type groups all numbers: both integers and reals. According to the context of the use of this *Numeric* type, it indicates either an integer, or a real attribute.

5.2 Constructed Attribute Types

The simple attribute types do not cover the whole attribute definition domain. Some objects are not constructed only from simple attribute types (*String, Integer, Boolean*).

For example, an *email* object is defined as the composition of a subject (*String*), a message (*String*) and the email addressee. Those addressee attributes are composed of a *String*, the @ character and the domain (*String*).

To express the addressee attributes in K-MADe, we used the *String* attribute type. However, the expression of the addressee type as a specific type provides information that can be used in order to design applications from task models.

In order to integrate types defined by K-MADe users, we add abstract object to the attribute type set. The definition of the email object according to these extensions is composed of three attributes: the subject (*String*), the message (*String*) and the email addressee (abstract object: email address). The *email address* type is defined as an abstract object composed by a name (*String*) and a domain name (*String*). Figure 6 represents the definition of both objects in UML representation.

Fig. 6. The UML representation of the *email* object definition (with only one addressee)

From the previous modifications, object attributes can have a String, a Numeric or a Boolean value. However, each attribute contains only one element. This condition is a limitation in the object description. For example, it implies the limitation of the email addressee number (only one addressee can be defined for each email while in the real world, emails may be sent to several persons). In order to express attributes that contain a set of entities (as the list of email addresses), we propose to add to the attribute type: collection of abstract objects. K-MAD defines collections, named *group* (list, stack...). We choose to use this concept as an additional constructed attribute type. Then, the new set of available types is: *Boolean, Numeric, String, Abstract Object* (one abstract object from the abstract object defined by user) and *Group* (one group from the groups defined by user).

6   Definition of Object Groups

In the K-MADe tool, "a group is a kind of structure (Stack, List, Set or Singleton) which consists in storing the instances of the same abstract object" (see Figure 2). Moreover, all concrete objects (instances) belong to a group. This definition, from the K-MADe user manual [11], restricts the object group definition and use.

We identify three limitations: first, the necessary adherence of concrete objects to a group, second, the composition of groups with only concrete objects (not any other entity) and third, the structures applied to range objects.

6.1   Concrete Object Independent from Any Group

From the K-MADe definition, a concrete object is composed of a *name, observation* about it and the *group* in which the concrete object will be stored. The name and the group are two mandatory attributes of the concrete object. Then, a concrete object can neither exist out a group nor in several groups.

By using K-MADe to express activities, we observe that some models use only one instance of an abstract object in the whole task model. For example, the description of the amount conversion activity brings in only one object for the conversion rate.

To express this single rate value, the designer has to define a group (a singleton group) (label 1 in Figure 7) and an object in this group (label 2 in Figure 7). This double definition is not intuitive for users [9] who cannot understand the semantics of a group that contain only one object. To semantically redefine K-MADe groups (in order to be conform to the usual semantic of group), we propose to modify the relation between group and concrete objects (Figure 8). This modification implies that the existence of concrete objects becomes independent of the defined groups and that a group is a container of several concrete objects.

Fig. 7. Definition of a unique instance of a concrete object

This relation modification makes it possible to define identical concrete objects as members of different groups. This double-membership may be mandatory to design some task models (for example, a person may be an employee and a customer of a shop).

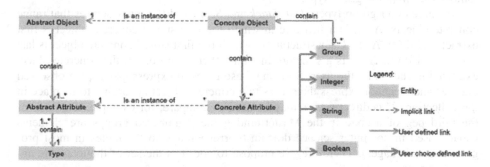

Fig. 8. Partial modified relations between abstract objects, concrete objects and groups

6.2 Group Composed of Objects of Several Types

Last, the definition of a group as a structure which stores concrete objects of only one abstract object, prevents the design of a group that contains objects of different types (such as a group that represents a basket with different articles). The modification of this relation between concrete object and group allows abstracting this relation as a characteristic between two independent entities. Then, a group contains concrete objects without any restriction due to its referenced abstract object. This notion may be expressed in object-oriented languages by inheritance [18] and the *select* type of EXPRESS [19] (definition of a type as a composition of several types).

6.3 Group Composed of Groups

A group entity is not only defined by a name and its aggregation type (list, set...) but also by the contained abstract object. This definition implies the expression of first class groups only. However, some groups may be collections of others. For example, most mailers propose to define folders that contain other folders that contain emails, as a folder "business relationship" composed of five folders corresponding to each current professional project.

In the current K-MADe tool version, the composition of collections of groups cannot be expressed. However, the modification of object definition that includes the group as an available attribute types (§ 6.2) provides an alternative description. In our example, the *emailFolders* group can contain the *emailProject1* group via a *project1Folder* object.

6.4 Aggregation Type

The K-MADe groups range objects. The available aggregation types that can define the object range in the groups are: *Singleton*, *List*, *Stack* and *Set*. The *singleton* aggregation type is dedicated to groups that contain only one object. This group type is mandatory to express the concrete objects that are not elements of a common-definition-group (only one instance of this object will be used in the whole task model). The definition of concrete objects independent of any group (see §6.1) prevents the need of a group that contains only one concrete object. Thus, we propose to remove the *Singleton* group type.

The three other group types (*List*, *Stack* and *Set*) are different structures that range concrete objects. A *list* is a structure in which the first stored concrete object is first extracted (FIFO). A *stack* is a structure in which the first stored concrete object is last extracted (LIFO). A *set* is a structure in which there is no order, the concrete object extracted is chosen by the user. By using these types to express groups, we observed that designers cannot express the access to a concrete object according to its place in the collection. This direct access may be used to compare, for example, the value of the third peg of a code in the Mastermind game. Numbered groups are elements usually used in computer science domain (corresponding to the tables in most programming languages). Therefore, we propose to add it in the set of the available aggregation types.

Though, the available group types necessary to express users' activities are: *list*, *stack*, *set* and *array*. However, these types are close to types used in computing and not to group categories used in the users' world. In order to cover these computing notions, we propose that K-MADe propose an assistant, to automatically affect the aggregation type to the collection according to the designer answers of several questions (Figure 9).

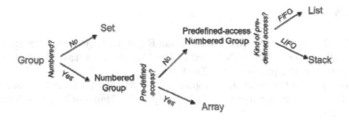

Fig. 9. Decision tree for kind of group

7 Conclusion and Future Work

Past research suggests the need to introduce objects in task model, especially when task models are used to produce interfaces [16, 20]. Nonetheless, they are rarely used in task modeling (as very few number of task models actually include objects). K-MADe is one tool that fully integrates objects in task modeling. In order to increase the expressive power of objects in task models, we studied their use to express user activities. From the design of five case studies, we observed that objects answer to some limitations (as the expression of thee deterministic choice). However, we observed also several other limitations and we proposed modifications in order to accommodate them. These modifications will improve the use of task models for designing interactive applications. For example, the capability to define object attributes as a collection of different other attributes (as the *addressee* object) allows developers to scent the presence of a specific computer object staying close to the user point of view. This evaluation highlights also the needs to integrate different formal description levels. For example, this progressive levels are illustrated by the proposition of a tool automatically identify the group type from user indications.

However, modifications on the kernel of the task model imply to add verification rules. For example, the addition of defined abstract objects as attribute type implies to verify that an object does not include itself. Moreover, some other modifications offer more freedom to designers. Research ought to be conducted in order to assure the added freedom does not decrease the model description. Furthermore, condition calculators (Figure 9) define functions that are applied to groups. We modified the group notion and the relationship between groups and objects so, the composition of the available functions set ought to be performed again.

While we tried to study interactive applications with the widest characteristics, we assume that our case studies are not representative of all interactive application types. For example, we do not particularly studied plastic interfaces [20]. The study of the K-MADe object expression coverage for the design of these specific applications should to be conducted. Moreover, we conducted our study in the design context, study has to be performed for the needs of other goals of task model use. Finally, once defined a complete K-MADe object module, evaluation of their use has to be planned.

References

1. Balbo, S., Ozkan, N., Paris, C.: Choosing the Right Task-modeling Notation: A Taxonomy. In: Diaper, D., Stanton, N.A. (eds.) The Handbook of Task Analysis for Human-Computer Interaction, pp. 445–466 (2004)
2. Limbourg, Q., Vanderdonckt, J.: Comparing Task Models for User Interface Design. In: Diaper, D. (ed.) The Handbook of Task Analysis for Human-Computer Interaction, pp. 135–154 (2004)
3. Sinning, D., Wurdel, M., Forbrig, P., Chalin, P., Khendek, F.: Practical Extensions for Task Models. In: Winckler, M., Johnson, H., Palanque, P. (eds.) TAMODIA 2007. LNCS, vol. 4849, pp. 42–55. Springer, Heidelberg (2007)
4. Paterno, F.: ConcurTaskTrees: An Engineered Notation for Task Models. In: Diaper, D., Stanton, N.A. (eds.) The Handbook of Task Analysis for Human-Computer Interaction, pp. 483–501 (2004)
5. Lucquiaud, V.: Proposition d'un noyau et d'une structure pour les modèles de tâches orientés utilisateurs. In: 17th French-speacking conference on Human-computer interaction, Toulouse, pp. 83–90 (2005)
6. Dix, A.: Tasks = Data + Action + Context: Automated Task Assistance through Data-Oriented Analysis (invited paper). In: Forbrig, P., Paternò, F. (eds.) HCSE/TAMODIA 2008. LNCS, vol. 5247, pp. 1–13. Springer, Heidelberg (2008)
7. Dittmar, A., Forbrig, P.: The influence of improved task models on dialogues. In: CADUI, pp. 1–14 (2004)
8. Van Der Veer, G.C.: GTA: Groupware Task Analysis - Modeling Complexity. Acta Psychologica, 297–322 (1996)
9. Caffiau, S., Girard, P., Scapin, D.L., Guittet, L., Sanou, L.: Assessment of Object Use for Task Modeling. In: Forbrig, P., Paternò, F. (eds.) HCSE/TAMODIA 2008. LNCS, vol. 5247, pp. 14–28. Springer, Heidelberg (2008)
10. Caffiau, S., Scapin, D.L., Sanou, L.: Retour d'Expérience en Enseignement de la Modélisation de Tâches. In: Proceedings of ERGO'IA, Biarritz, pp. 135–143 (2008)
11. K-MADe electronic reference, http://kmade.sourceforge.net/
12. Gamboa, R.F., Scapin, D.L.: Editing MAD* task description for specifying user interfaces, at both semantic and presentation levels. In: Harrison, M.D., Torres, J.C. (eds.) Eurographics Workshop on Design, Specification and Verification of Interactive Systems (DSV-IS 1997), Granada, Spain, pp. 193–208 (1997)
13. Scapin, D., Bastien, J.-M.C.: Analyse des tâches et aide ergonomique à la conception: l'approche MAD* (chapitre 3). In: Kolski, C. (ed.) Analyse et conception de l'I.H.M. / Interaction Homme-Machine pour les S.I., Paris, France, vol. 1 (2001)
14. Lucquiaud, V.: Sémantique et Outil pour la Modélisation des Tâches Utilisateur: N-MDA. Thesis. Poitiers, p. 285 (2005)
15. AMBOSS electronic reference, http://wwwcs.uni-paderborn.de/cs/ag-szwillus/lehre/ws05_06/PG/PGAMBOSS
16. Paternò, F., Santoro, C.: One model, many interfaces. In: Kolski, C., Vanderdonckt, J. (eds.) Computer-Aided Design of User Interfaces (CADUI 2002), Valenciennes, France, pp. 143–154 (2002)
17. Bellatreche, L., Boukhalfa, K., Caffiau, S.: ParAdmin: Un Outil d'Assistance à l'Administration et Tuning d'un Entrepôt de Données. In: EDA 2008, Toulouse (2008)
18. The Unified Modeling Language, http://www.uml.org/
19. Express: The EXPRESS language reference manual
20. Calvary, G., Coutaz, J., Thevenin, D., Limbourg, Q., Bouillon, L., Vanderdonckt, J.: A unifying reference framework for multi-target user interfaces. Interacting With Computers 15(3), 289–308 (2003)

iUCP – Estimating Interaction Design Projects with Enhanced Use Case Points

Nuno Jardim Nunes

University of Madeira, Lab:USE, Campus da Penteada,
9000-390 Funchal, Portugal
njn@uma.pt

Abstract. This paper describes an approach to adapt the use-case point estimation method to fit the requirements of agile development of interactive software. Creating product cost estimates early in the development lifecycle is a challenge for the software industry, they require substantial data from past projects and constant feedback and fine-tuning, which are rarely available or consistent through interactive software development. In addition, the profusion of incremental and evolutionary development methods (like Scrum and XP) produced new challenges with estimating frequent releases. Here we propose several changes to the original use-case point estimation method, in particular to take advantage of the enhanced information that can be extracted from usage-centered design (usageCD) that devotes particular attention to critical aspects like weighting actors and uses-cases for complexity. We propose to exploit user-roles, essential use-cases and the usageCD architecture to enhance the weighting heuristics for assigning complexity factors to actors and use-cases required to calculate the unadjusted use-case point reflecting the complexity of the requirements for a given iteration or evolution. We propose to exploit user-roles as the main basis for weighting complex actors, which originally are grouped in the highest weight factor. Conversely we propose to extract the complexity of use-cases from essential use case steps depicted through user intentions and system responsibilities and also the analysis classes extract from those for the usageCD architecture. Detailing this approach the paper presents a contribution, not only to leverage more accurate early lifecycle software estimation, but also to bridge the gap between SE and HCI enabling cross-fertilization between the two disciplines.

Keywords: Software estimation, use-cases, interaction design, integrating SE and HCI.

1 Introduction

For several years the software engineering (SE) and human-computer interaction (HCI) communities tried to bridge methods and techniques that are successful in either software development or interaction design. The cross-fertilization of both disciplines is hard. Methods and techniques are developed independently and are underused mostly because we lack a common understanding between the two communities. Despite that

D. England et al. (Eds.): TAMODIA 2009, LNCS 5963, pp. 131–145, 2010.

practitioners are increasingly required to work together in multidisciplinary teams, examples of the lack of communication in both disciplines are evident in the major conferences. For instance at CHI'2008 several workshops, panels and special sessions discussed the impact of agile methods in interaction design and in particular how to integrate user-centered design (UCD) techniques in the software development lifecycle. This is more than 10 years after agile development was coined in the SE field and more than 20 years since the early agile methods emerged in the mid 80s (for instance Scrum [1]). On the opposite direction many UCD methods and techniques that are mature and used successfully in the HCI community are unknown and unrecognized by software developers. Although these techniques tackle precisely the major problems of SE (requirements and user-involvement) they are not recognized as suitable and powerful by software practitioners and are still far from large-scale adoption.

In [2] Seffah and Metzer discussed the obstacles and myths of usability and software engineering. The authors argue that we need to educate software and usability engineers to work together, and tackle communication issues that prevent cross-pollinating of disciplines. For instance the fact that usability is a confusing concept and filling the gap between HCI and SE impacts the organization models. These are all outstanding issues that will require a lot of effort and are mostly based on a restrictive vision that decouples the user-interface from the remaining system and builds a barrier between SD and UI specialists. This results in parallel UCD and SE processes that don't communicate and influence each other preventing the whole to become much more than the mere sum of the parts. Here we discuss how one popular and important SE technique for creating product cost estimates early in the development lifecycle through the popular use-case point method. Early estimates are an important challenge for the SD industry and we argue that bringing an HCI insight to this SE technique is not only beneficial for the accuracy of the estimation, but also a basic way to bridge the gap between HCI and SE early in the lifecycle. In this paper we argue that for interactive system development early estimates based on models of requirements can only be accurate if they reflect the HCI concerns related to users and their interaction with the system.

2   Use Case Points (UCP)

Several estimating models have been proposed in the SE field over the years, notably Function Point Analysis (FPA) and Constructive Cost Model [3]. FPA was pioneered by Albrecht in 1977 and assigns a point to each function in an application further adjusting them for the product environmental factors, like complexity of technical issues, developer skills and risk. The Constructive Cost Model (also known as CO-COMO) uses statistical returns to calculate project cost and duration within a given probability. Boehm proposed this model in 1981 to provide a tool for predictably estimate product cost and is still evolving today under the sponsorship of the Center for Systems and Software Engineering at USC. The underlying assumption of both FPA and COCOMO is that statistically significant historical data exists to drive the factoring of the models. However companies find very hard to find a consistent definition of functions and environmental factors across multiple projects and development platforms.

With the advent of object-oriented software engineering use-cases emerged as the dominant technique for structuring requirements. This technique pioneered by Jacobson was further integrated in the Unified Modeling Language (UML) and the commercial Rational Unified Process (RUP) thus becoming a de facto standard for requirements modeling in the SE field. Later Karner, also from Rational, created a software estimation technique that assigns points to use-cases in much the same way that FPA assign points to functions [4]. This technique was named Use-Case Points (UCP) and also integrated in the Rational Unified Process receiving tool support from the tools provided by the company at IBM and from other popular UML tool vendors.

The UCP model became popular due to its relative simplicity and rather high level that makes it a good candidate as a method for early estimation of software size and effort. In the following sub-sections we briefly discuss the UCP model based on the original model presented by Schneider and Winters [5]. We refrain from discussing the notion of actor and use-case at this stage and thus adopt the standard UML definitions [6]:

- Use case – A use case is the specification of a set of actions performed by a system, which yields an observable result that is, typically, of value for one or more actors or other stakeholders of the system.
- Actor – An actor specifies a role played by a user or any other system that interacts with the subject.

These definitions are the starting point of the model since the main activity of UCP is to estimate the complexity of actors and use-cases. The term estimation is not accidental because building a use-case model under given circumstances requires several assumptions that improve over time according to experience and statistically significant data across projects and organizations.

2.1 Estimating Use Case Points

The use-case point method starts by determining the unadjusted actor weight (UAW). For each actor in the use-case model we attribute a weight factor based on the following heuristics:

- Simple actors (factor 1) – system actors that communicate to the system through an API;
- Average actors (factor 2) – system actors that communicate to the system through a protocol or data store;
- Complex actors (factor 3) – human actors interacting normally through a GUI or other human interface;

The total unadjusted actor weight is thus the weighted sum of all the actors in the use-case model. For example if we have a system with 3 simple actors, 2 average actors and 1 complex actor, the total: UAW = 3*1 + 2*2 + 1*3 = 10. Obviously accurate classification of actors needs to be backup up by feedback from historical data from past projects.

After weighting the actors a similar process is applied to use-cases. For each use-case we determine the weight factor of simple, average and complex. Again the method defines a heuristic based on use-case transactions and implementation information:

- Simple use-cases (factor 5) – simple user interface or processing, touches only one database entity, the success scenario involves 3 or fewer transactions and the implementation 5 or less classes;
- Average use-case (factor 10) – moderate user interface or processing, touches 2 or 3 database entities, the success scenario involves 4 to 7 transactions and the implementation 5 to 10 classes;
- Complex use-cases (factor 15) – complex user interface or processing, touches 3 or more database entities, the success scenario involves more than 7 transactions and the implementation more than 10 classes;

The total unadjusted use-case weight (UUCW) is thus the weighted sum of all the use-cases in the use case model. For example if the system involves 3 simple, 2 average and 1 complex use-cases then the total UUCW = 3*5 + 2*10 + 1*15 = 60. Adding the total for actors and use-cases leads to the unadjusted use-case points (UUCP), in the example provide the total UUCP = UAW + UUCW = 10 + 60 = 70.

The UUCP is further modified to reflect the complexity of the project and experience level of the development. This is accomplished through weighting technical and environmental factors, given by the Technical Complexity Factor (TCF) and the Environment Complexity Factor (ECF). For the TCF we assign a perceived complexity value (between 0 and 5) to a series of 13 technical factors. Conversely the ECF is estimated assigning a complexity value (also between 0 and 5) to 13 environmental (or sometimes called experience factors). It is not our goal here to discuss in detail these factors as we are concentrating on weighting actors and use-cases. For a comprehensive discussion of the UCP method please refer to [4, 5].

The following summarizes the calculations required to calculate the final UCP for a given project:

$$UCP = UUCP \times TCF \times ECF \qquad (1)$$

$$UUCP = UUCW + UAW \qquad (2)$$

$$TCF = C_1 + C_2 \sum_{i=1}^{13} W_i \times F_i, \text{ where } C_1 \text{ and } C_2 \text{ are constants } (C_1 = 0,6 \text{ and} \qquad (3)$$

$C_2 = 0,01$), W is the weight attributed to the F perceived complexity factor.

$$ECF = C_1 + C_2 \sum_{i=1}^{13} W_i \times F_i, \text{ where } C_1 \text{ and } C_2 \text{ are constants } (C_1 = 1,4 \text{ and} \qquad (4)$$

$C_2 = -0,03$), W is the weight attributed to the F perceived complexity factor.

After estimating the total UCP the total estimated number of hours for the project is determined by multiplying the UCP by a productivity factor (PF), which defines the ratio of development man-hours per use case point. PF is based on past project statistics or by establishing a baseline from the UCP of previously completed projects. A value between 15 and 30 is considered typical depending on the team's overall experience. For example taking our example value of UUCP = UAW + UUCW = 10 + 60 = 70, and considering TCF=1.02 and ECF=1.04 the total UCP=70 * 1.02 * 1.04 =

74.256 and applying a PF of 20 yields to a total estimate of 1 485.12 man.hours for the project.

2.2 Related Work

The previous section describes the calculations required to perform an early estimation based on the UCP method. The calculations themselves do not represent any difficulty; the central problem is defining the elements of the model (actors and use cases) and assigning weights to them. In [6] Dieve provides a comprehensive discussion of several issues related to weighting actors and use-cases, in particular the author argues that to obtain reasonably accurate estimates we need to reflect in the use-case model some aspects of the existing applications and project, including some clarifications of the concept or actor and use case across and within projects. In this section we briefly review several of Dieve's issues and then build on them to the domain of interactive software products and interaction design.

- Use case transactions. As we discussed in the previous section the complexity of use-cases is based on the concept of use-case transaction. Dieve formulates this based on the concept of elementary process, meaning that a use-case transaction is the smallest unit of activity that is meaningful from an actor's point of view. A use-case transaction is self-contained and leaves the business of the application sized in a consistent state. A differentiation is required between a use-case transaction and a use-case scenario, the former can contain more that one scenario and vice-versa;
- Scoping. Another important issue is related to the fact that although use-cases are a requirements modeling technique, and thus should not include design concerns, in order to obtain accurate estimates they should reflect some aspects of the conceptual design of the project. Hence the selection of actors may be dictated by the properties of a project, i.e., business concerns and other forms of additional information about actors have an impact in weighting actor complexity, which is not considered in the initial formulation of the UCP method.
- Zero-Weight. An additional important issue is that some actors and use-cases could be excluded from the estimation model. Actors that don't reflect any significant interaction with the system will not impact the project effort. Use-cases can also be zero-weighted because they don't generate an implementation, i.e., some functionality can be provided programmatically and although conceptually they are useful at the requirements level they don't impact the estimation and should be excluded from the calculations;
- Granularity. Since use-cases structure the requirements the issue of granularity becomes very important because for an accurate estimation we have to ensure some uniform sizing. This is particularly relevant when use-cases include much more than the higher complexity limit heuristic of 8 transactions and 10 implementation classes, i.e., not partitioning use-cases that are significantly higher than these limits ignores their real size;

Many other issues could occur when a use case model is used for estimation. The central issue is that use-case estimation relies on the quality of the underlying use-case model, in particular ensuring a consistent application of the heuristics across and within projects. Despite the controversy about estimation methods, in [8] Carroll describes how a large multi-team software engineering organization estimates project cost accurately and early in the software development lifecycle using UCP and the process of evaluating metrics to ensure the accuracy of the model. Although the above discussion applies to general software system development, many issues are clearly related to user-centered design concepts, like models of users (actors) and of interaction (use-cases and transactions). In the remainder of this paper we explore how HCI techniques can inform and guide the estimation heuristics in a way that is not only consistent with interaction design practice, but also highly relevant to sustain several heuristics across projects.

3   iUCP – Estimating Actors and Use-Cases in Interaction Design Projects

For the purpose of explaining how interaction design can influence estimation of use-case points we consider the model-based techniques pioneered by Larry Constantine [8] and further expanded by colleagues [10, 11] at the Laboratory for Usage-centered Software Engineering (Lab:USE) at the University of Madeira. Although many other techniques are used in design practice (for instance [12]), they usually don't leverage techniques that are popular in the software engineering field, in particular use-cases and user-roles. Constantine's approach is currently named activity-based design in an evolution of the original usage-centered design [9]. The distinction between usage-centered and user-centered design is a matter of emphasis than an absolute difference in perspective. They are both methods that combine field studies, user involvement and modeling. However, in activity or usage-centered design models are in the forefront and drive development that is then evaluated through user studies. On the contrary user-centered design methods rely more on user studies and feedback. It is out of the scope of this paper to discuss the implications of the emphasis in both approaches, we provide examples from activity-centered design because this paper reports our experience applying those methods and producing estimations from a consistent sample of projects. The fact that usage (or activity) based design is more narrowly focused on user performance and on the creation of tools to enhance the efficiency and dependability of user performance is not detriment of the application of the same techniques to other user-centered design methods given that they are used to produce some for of requirements models based on use-cases.

In the following subsections we discuss the implications of these methods in weighting actors and use cases.

3.1   Weighting Actors

Effective interaction design involves understanding users and their needs. Like in the conventional UML and UP tradition, in usage-centered design users who interact with a system are referred to as actors. However, unlike conventional UML the concept of actor is expanded through user roles, an additional abstraction representing a relationship between users and a system. According to Constantine, in its simplest form, a

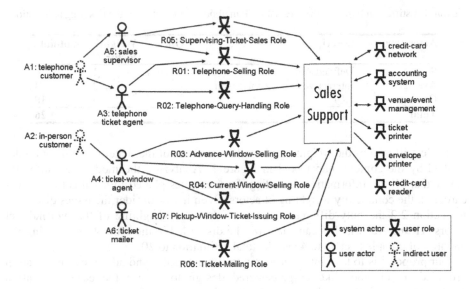

R01 - Current-Sales-and-Ticketing Role

context (of role performance): isolated in booth, likely facing queue of customers; final step in performance promotion and sales

characteristics (of role performance): relatively simple task performed repeatedly with some training, prior experience likely; performed under some time pressure, which increases as show time approaches

criteria (for support of role performance): simplified, highly efficient interaction; foolproof means of identifying customer, guarantee that all the right tickets are dispensed and received by the customer

Fig. 1. Context map for an example ticketing application (taken from [12]), on the top is the user role map including several actors and their supporting roles and the detail description of the *Current-Sales-and-Ticketing Role*

role can be described by the context in which it is performed, the characteristic manner in which it is performed, and by the evident design criteria for effective support of performance of the role [13]. An example from [13] is shown bellow, both in terms of the underlying context map (an adapted form of a UML use-case diagram) and the detailed user-role description for the *Current-Sales-and-Ticketing Role*.

The difference between a context map produced by the usage-centered design method and a conventional use case model is abyssal in terms of the richness of the information conveyed about the complexity underlying each actor. Considering that a conventional UML model would represent this problem with 12 actors (A1 to A6 and 6 system actors) and applying the original UCP method the estimation would be 4 simple actors (credit card reader, envelope printer, ticket printer, venue/event manager), 2 average actors (credit-card network, accounting system) and 6 complex actors (A1 to A6).

Table 1. Estimation based on the original UCP method for the actors in the ticketing application

Actor type	Description	Qnty	Weight factor	Subtotal
Simple	Defined API	4	1	4
Average	Interactive or protocol driven	2	2	4
Complex	GUI	6	3	18
Total				**26**

Table 1 illustrates the weighting of the 12 use-cases of the ticketing application de-scribed by the context map model in Figure 1. Analyzing the model we can easily verify that all the information regarding the user-roles played by each actor are dis-carded in the complexity weighting of actors. Even if we consider the issues discussed in section 2.2 the only difference would be the zero weighting of the two indirect actors A1 and A2, which means they will be discarded in the estimation reducing the quantity of complex actors to 4 and the total estimation to 20.

Our proposal is to take into consideration the user roles and additional information provided by methods like usage-centered design to inform the early estimation through the weighting of the actors. Clearly the number of roles supported by each actor provides an important way to infer the complexity associated with each actor and consequently the weigh factor that should be applied. Additionally usage-centered design suggest the concept of focal role together with several relationships that make up a model designated user role map (check [13] for a detailed discussion). Focal roles are roles recognized as particularly important for a successful design, they serve a central focus to the rest of the design process, but not to the exclusion of other user roles [13].

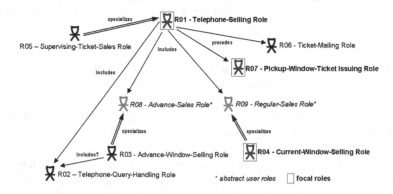

Fig. 2. User role map for an example ticketing application (taken from [13]), focal roles are highlighted

Our experience working and consulting on several projects applying usage-centered design methods suggests the following revised heuristics for actor weighting in interactive software projects:

- Simple system actors (factor 1) – system actors that communicate to the system through an API;
- Average system actors (factor 2) – system actors that communicate to the system through a protocol or data store;
- Simple human actors (factor 3) – human actors interacting with the system supported by one user role;
- Average human actors (factor 4) – human actors interacting with the system supported by 2 or 3 user roles or a single focus role;
- Complex human actors (factor 5) – human actors interacting with the system supported by more than 3 user roles or more than one focus role;

Table 2. Estimation based on the modified iUCP method for the actors in the ticketing application provided in Figures 2 and 3

Actor type	Description	Qnty	Weight factor	Subtotal
Simple system	Defined API	4	1	4
Average system	Interactive or protocol driven	2	2	4
Simple human	Support one user role	1	3	3
Average human	Support 2-3 user roles or 1 focal role	2	4	8
Complex human	Support more than 3 user roles or more than 1 focus role	1	5	5
Total				**24**

As we can see from Table 2 the human actors are now divided into simple, human and complex with respectively weight factors of 3, 4 and 5. The analysis of the examples provided in Figure 1 and 2 following the revised heuristics for iUCP suggest the following classification:

- A1 – indirect actor, zero-weighted (0)
- A2 – indirect actor, zero-weighted (0)
- A3 – supports 2 roles (R01 and R02) one focal – average human actor (4)
- A4 – supports 3 roles (R03, R04, R07) two focal – complex human actor (5)
- A5 – supports 2 roles (R01 and R02) one focal – average human actor (4)
- A6 – supports 1 role (R06) not focal- simple human actor (3)
- A7 – A12 – are system actors, 4 simple and 2 average according to the initial weighting which doesn't change on iUCP

From the above classification we can conclude that in a simple example there is a total difference of four use case points (from 20 to 24) based on the revised actor weighting (assuming both approaches zero-weight the indirect actors). Although this difference might look insignificant in a real-world project with three times more actors and roles the impact is far from being neglectful. But our experience shows that more important than the calculation itself; the iUCP revised heuristics provide systematic guidance that prevents many of the problems indentified by Dieve in [8]. The original method simply classifies human-actors with the same weight factor which is arguable a consistent heuristic for interactive applications that usually have one or two system actors and more than one dozen human-actors. By assigning the majority of the actors with the same complexity weight factor the UCP method becomes arguable useful for interactive system development.

3.2 Weighting Use-Cases

Since their introduction by Jacobson in object-oriented software engineering, use cases have enjoyed a seemingly explosive growth to become ubiquitous in both development methods and development practice [14]. Part of their success can be attributed to the simplicity of the concept itself but probably also a consequence of their imprecise definition. In fact entire books and thesis have been devoted to the discussion of what a use-case is and we can find many instantiations of use-case descriptions that vary in scope, detail, focus, format, structure and style. It is not our purpose here to discuss use-cases, a thorough albeit controversial discussion can be found in [14].

It seems obvious that an estimation method relying on weighting use-cases will suffer from the same uncertainty that we can find in the literature about using the concept to structure requirements. However, in usage-centered design they are clearly defined through the pioneering and fundamental concept of essential use-cases [14]. Unlike conventional uses cases, defined in the UML specification (see section 2), essential use cases are define by Constantine [14] as:

> "a single, discrete, complete, meaningful, and well-defined task of interest to an external user in some specific role or roles in relationship to a system, comprising the user intentions and system responsibilities in the course of accomplishing that task, described in abstract, technology-free, implementation-independent terms using the language of the application domain and of external users in role".

The difference between the two definitions is not subtle as much as the consequences for designing interactive systems. Not only essential use-cases are more abstract, generalized and technology-free descriptions of the essence of a given problem, but also more importantly they are described in a systematic sequence of steps divided between user intentions and system responsibilities. The essential nature of these steps provides a systematic way of identifying transactions, which are key to classify use-cases in the UCP method. The problem is better explained through a example. Bellow is a popular example provided in textbooks for the UML describing a use-case for withdrawing cash (taken from the EPF wiki at www.eclipse.org):

1. *The use case begins when Bank Customer inserts their Bank Card.*
2. *Use Case: Validate User is performed.*
3. *The ATM displays the different alternatives that are available on this unit. In this case the Bank Customer always selects "Withdraw Cash".*
4. *The ATM prompts for an account. See Supporting Requirement SR-yyy for account types that shall be supported.*
5. *The Bank Customer selects an account.*
6. *The ATM prompts for an amount.*
7. *The Bank Customer enters an amount.*
8. *Card ID, PIN, amount and account is sent to Bank as a transaction. The Bank Consortium replies with a go/no go reply telling if the transaction is ok.*

9. *Then money is dispensed*
10. *The Bank Card is returned.*
11. *The receipt is printed*
12. *The use case ends successfully*

According to the original UCP heuristics this use-case will likely be classified as complex since it involves arguably more than 7 transactions. However when we look at the essential use-case counterpart description, the number of essential steps is much different. Bellow we have 2 "essential transactions" (system responsibilities), which would classify this use case as simple. The discrepancy is vast and questionably the reason underneath the problems applying UCP across companies, teams and even projects. Interestingly enough the heuristics for assigning weight factors to use-cases are highly dependent on assumptions about the user-interface. In section 2.1 a simple use case corresponded to a simple user interface, an average to a moderate user interface and a complex use-case to a complex user interface. However conventional use cases don't reflect the division between user intentions and system responsibilities that conveys the notion of interaction (i.e. a interaction happens when a user specifies an intention to the system).

User intention	*System responsibility*
identify self	
	check identity
specify amount	
	provide cash

Indeed, in usage-centered design an essential use case represents a single, discrete intention carried out by a user in some role. This provides a systematic way of expressing transactions as steps in a dialog in which user intentions and system responsibilities are abstract, simplified, and stripped of all assumptions about technology or implementation. Originally this form of description was intended to get closer to the essence of the task from the perspective of the user in a role, thus avoiding unintended or premature assumptions about the user interface to be designed [14]. When applied to estimating use-cases it becomes an important way to retain scope and prevent the granularity problems described in section 2.2.

However estimating transactions is not the only concern when assigning weight factors to use-cases. The heuristics specifically mention two additional criteria depending on the conceptual architecture: (i) the number of entities manipulated in the context of the use case and, (ii) the number of classes implementing the use case. The relationship between use-cases and implementation classes is accomplished in the UML convention using the entity/control/boundary pattern. However this pattern doesn't reflect the separation of concerns required for interactive system development, boundary classes encapsulate both interface to human actors and system actors and thus there is no clear distinction between human and system interaction. As a consequence the implementation classes extracted from the use-cases will not reflect the complexity of the user-interface, which is key to sustain the assignment of weight factors to use-cases.

In [15] we proposed an extension of this framework to include two important concepts that reflect the user intentions that form the basis of usage-centered design: tasks and interaction spaces. Therefore, the boundary-control-entity pattern is extended with additional task and interaction space class stereotypes:

– <<task>> classes that are used to model the structure of the dialogue between the user and the system in terms of meaningful and complete sets of actions required to achieve a goal; and

– <<interaction space>> classes are used to represent the space within the user interface of a system where the user interacts with all the functions, containers, and information needed for carrying out some particular task or set of interrelated tasks.

In [16] we described how to extract the extended architecture from the essential use-cases. The process is highlighted in Fig. 3, where <<task>> classes originate from user intentions, <<control>> and <<entity>> classes from the system responsibilities and finally <<interaction spaces>> from the crossing of both. This process not only increases the traceability in usage-centered design but becomes central to identify the number of entities and overall classes required to implement a given use-case. In addition, and contrary to the conventional UML approach, the architecture reflects the "complexity" of the structure of use which will eventually originate the user-interface, hence it provides a mechanism to map the complexity of the UI to the use-cases which is not achievable with the original method.

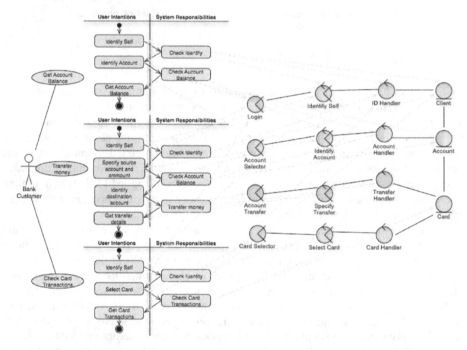

Fig. 3. A conceptual architecture extracted from essential use cases (taken from [16])

The example provided in Fig. 3 for an ATM system illustrates how the usage-centered design architecture can be used to inform the classification of use-cases in the iUCP method. Unlike the heuristics applied to weight actors we don't propose to change the weighting factors for the use-cases, but simply introduce the usage-centered design concepts of essential transaction and implementation class described previously. Therefore transactions are conceived as the total number of system responsibilities identified in a given essential use-case and conversely implementation classes are considered as the total number of classes originating from an essential use case according to the approached described in [16] depicted in Fig. 3 through the dashed lines connecting the use-case descriptions to the conceptual architecture.

Table 3. Estimation based on the modified iUCP method for the use-cases in the ATM application example provide in Fig. 3

Use case type	Description	Qnty	Weight factor	Subtotal
Simple	Simple UI, 1 entity, ≤3 transactions	0	5	0
Average	Average UI, 2-3 entities, 4-7 transactions	1	10	10
Complex	Complex UI, >3 entities, >7 transactions	2	15	30
Total				40

As we can see from Table 3 for a small example it is clear how to apply the heuristics when considering the small example provided in Fig. 3. We simply count the number of system responsibilities and user intentions per use case and the number of originating implementation classes. This contrasts the uncertainty that we could envision from starting with a conventional use case. Not only it is harder to isolate transactions but there is little guidance regarding the number of implementation classes corresponding to each use case and in particular reflecting the complexity of the UI.

4 Conclusions and Future Work

In this paper we described iUCP, a modified version of the use-case point software estimation method that leverages the techniques from usage-centered design to improve the heuristics traditionally used in Software Engineering to create product cost estimates early in the development lifecycle. Early estimation of software is critical industry challenge and we argue that our approach not only helps bridge the gap between SE and HCI but also accomplished that providing software development with useful systematic guidance towards producing early estimates for software based products. With the profusion of agile incremental and evolutionary approaches used in interactive software development it is increasingly important to find ways to enable both HCI and SE experts to collaborate early in the lifecycle. By proposing to use key usage-centered development techniques - like use roles, essential use-cases and interactive conceptual architectural models - we not only bridge the gap between SE and HCI but more importantly illustrate how HCI techniques can be useful in traditional engineering practice of software development like estimation and models.

The ability to accurately predict the cost of a project early in the lifecyle is a major differentiator for the software industry. The capability of combining SE and HCI, enables cross-fertilization between the two disciplines and encourages new ways of collaboration between interaction designers and software developers. This brings a new perspective to developers because they can foresee the advantage of using HCI techniques early in the lifecycle. Conversely interaction designers can better understand the impact of their models of users and recognize the impact of UI elements at the architecture level, building common ground for other activities like prioritizing development and planning releases.

The iUCP method was developed building on statistical data from usage-centered development projects were the author consulted and worked in the past years. However, a systematic evaluation at the metric level requires extensive data collection and analysis over the course of years. Our remit here is not to evidence the validity of the estimation method, which can be found elsewhere (for instance in [8]). The adaptations of the UCP method are minimal so that we can preserve the integrity of the original model. Our goal with the iUCP adaptation of the method is to help both software developers and interaction designers to apply heuristics that are suitable for interactive applications and work consistently across and within projects. We have taught and applied the iUCP method both in graduated SE and HCI courses with good results in terms of student's capability to accurately estimate cost and effort of interactive applications. We have also backtracked iUCP on several real-world projects against actual data of development effort and cost with good results. We are currently planning to develop an empirical study that could validate the results against standard UCP, and also plan to provide automated tool support for iUCP.

References

1. Takeuchi, H., Nonaka, I.: The New New Product Development Game (PDF). Harvard Business Review (January-February 1986)
2. Seffah, A., Metzker, E.: The Obstacles and Myths of Usability and Software Engineering. Communications of the ACM 47(12), 71–76 (2004)
3. Boehm, B.: Software engineering economics. Prentice-Hall, Englewood Cliffs (1981)
4. Karner, G.: Resource Estimation for Objectory Projects. Objective Systems SFAB (1993)
5. Schneider, G., Winters, J.P.: Applying Use Cases: A Practical Guide. Addison-Wesley, Reading (1998)
6. OMG: The UML superstructure, http://www.uml.org
7. Dieve, S.: Use cases modeling and software estimation: Applying Use Case Points. ACM Software Engineering Notes 31(6) (2006)
8. Carrol, E.: Estimating Software Based on Use Case Points (2002)
9. Constantine, L.L., Lockwood, L.A.D.: Software for use: a practical guide to the models and methods of usage-centered design. Addison Wesley, Longman (1999)
10. Nunes, N.J., Cunha, J.F.: Wisdom: A Software Engineering Method for Small Software Development Companies. IEEE Software 17, 113–119 (2000)
11. Nunes, N.J., Cunha, J.F.: Whitewater Interactive System Development with Object Models. In: Harmelen, M. (ed.) OOUID. Addison-Wesley, Reading (2001)
12. Cooper, A.: About Face 3.0: The Essentials of Interaction Design. Wiley, Chichester (2007)
13. Constantine, L.: Users, Roles, and Personas. In: Pruitt, Aldin (eds.) The Persona Lifecycle. Morgan-Kaufmann, San Francisco (2006)

14. Constantine, L., Lockwood, L.: Structure and Style in Use Cases for User Interface Design. In: van Harmelen, M. (ed.) OOUID. Addison-Wesley, Reading (2001)
15. Nunes, N., Cunha, J.F.: Towards a UML profile for interactive systems development: the Wisdom approach. In: Evans, A., Kent, S., Selic, B. (eds.) UML 2000. LNCS, vol. 1939, pp. 101–116. Springer, Heidelberg (2000)
16. Nunes, N.: What Drives Software Development: Bridging the Gap Between Software and Usability Engineering. Human Computer Interaction Series. Springer, Heidelberg (2008)

Agent-Based User Interface Generation from Combined Task, Context and Domain Models

Vi Tran[1], Manuel Kolp[1], Jean Vanderdonckt[1], Yves Wautelet[1],
and Stéphane Faulkner[2]

[1] Louvain School of Management-PRISME, Université catholique de Louvain,
Louvain-la-Neuve, Belgium
{Vi.Tran,Manuel.Kolp,Jean.Vanderdonckt,
Yves.Wautelet}@uclouvain.be
[2] Louvain School of Management-PRISME, University of Namur, Louvain-la-Neuve, Belgium
Stephane.Faulkner@fundp.ac.be

Abstract. User interfaces (UI) for data systems has been a technical and human interaction research question for a long time. Today these user interfaces require dynamic automation and run-time generation to properly deal with on a large-scale. This paper presents an agent-based framework, i.e., a methodological process, a meta-model and a computer software to drive the automatic database user interface design and code behind generation from the task model, context model and domain model combined together. This includes both the user interface and the basic functions of the database application.

Keywords: Task Model, Domain Model, Context Model, Automatic Generation, User Interface, Agent Software.

1 Introduction

Automatic user interface generation has been investigated by numerous Human Computer Interaction (HCI) research works due to its capability and importance in the UI development process providing benefits such as low-cost and rapid implementation. There are currently numerous and various approaches using different input materials to automate UI generation such as techniques based on architectural designs, design patterns, use-case scenarios, declarative models[2, 3, 4].

In order to generate user interface, models are usually not used independently from other ones. For instance, TOOL[4] combines the task and user models; GOLIATH [2] combines the application, presentation and dialogue models together to generate the user interface; other research generate automatically the user interface from combining the domain and use case models [5]. Combining models is, as a matter of fact, an important concept in UI generation: the different models describe different aspects of the user interface [7] and serve specific purposes at different stages of the design process.

This research hence proposes a framework, i.e., a methodological process, a meta model and a software to drive the automatic database user interface design and code behind generation from the task, domain and context models combined together.

Our framework is based and supported by declarative technologies. More specifically, we will adopt the agent paradigm (models, language, methods, ...) to analyze

D. England et al. (Eds.): TAMODIA 2009, LNCS 5963, pp. 146–161, 2010.

task, context and domain models and generate the user interface specifications and application code.

The rest of this paper is organized as follows: we present, in Section 2, the motivation of this research. In Section 3, we proposes our automatic UI and code generation process taken together the task, context and domain. Section 4 explains the roles of the main agents that participate in this process such as the query analyzer, the UI designer, the code generator for both the data reviewing and editing. Finally, we propose some conclusions and plan for future work.

2 Motivation

This section motivates use of the Task, Context and Domain models to generate the UI and Application codes and presents what is an agent systems.

2.1 Multi-model Analysis

Two main reasons justify the automatic generation of user interfaces from task, domain and context models. The first one is the commonality of these models: in order to develop a software system, the developer usually starts with building the task, domain and context models so that it is convenient to generate UI on the basis of these existing resources. The second one belongs to the nature of the models itself; indeed they are inherently part of the UI design, more precisely:

- The task model expresses how a end user may want to interact with a system in order to reach a given goal; this expression is intended to be independent of any particular implementation or technology. This explains why a same set of models could initiate several different user interfaces. Therefore, the task model is used to specify a generic user interface.
- The domain model defines the aspects of the application which can be adapted or which are otherwise required for the running of the system. Therefore, the domain model is used to specify the control of this user interface – at this level the user interface is specified in more detail.
- The context model describes the user abilities, the environment in which the user works and the platform that can be used for interacting with the system [11]. Therefore, the context model is used to influence the design and to select among alternative solutions in the design space.

2.2 Forward Engineering: Code Generation

Most of the research works have only focused on the user interface generation and omits the importance of the application code generation. To produce an accurate application at low cost, the developers expect that both the user interface and the application code are automatically generated. The application code is generated to perform the generic tasks of the database application, especially, those tasks related to editing, inserting, deleting and searching data.

The present research focuses on the application code generation for the tasks of a data-oriented application in the following context:

- When the demand for data manipulation is very high. Data manipulations are regularly repeated in most database applications especially for common tasks such as those listed above.
- When functions are easily performed through receiving data from the user, displaying data to the user, executing the different SQL select, insert, update and delete queries for the different user requirements.

2.3 Agent Systems: A Definition

An agent is a declarative entity defined as "a computer system, situated in some environment that is capable of flexible autonomic action in order to meet its design objective" [8]. The declarative nature of an agent can be characterized by its autonomy, flexibility and situateness [9]. The autonomy of agents reflects their social and decentralized nature. The flexible way in which agents operate to accomplish their goals is particularly suited to these business systems which are normally expected to function in an ever-changing environment. The situateness implicitly supposes that agents are not useful as stand-alone entities. As a matter of fact, they are most of the time structured in a multi-agent system (MAS).

The global behavior of a MAS derives from the interaction between the constituent agents: they cooperate, coordinate or negotiate with one another. A multi-agent system is then considered a society of autonomous, collaborative, and goal-driven software components, the agents, like a social organization. The agents intelligently and automatically behave and collaborate to fulfill the objectives of a declarative structure [6]. Each role that an agent has the ability to play has a well defined set of responsibilities (goals) achieved by means of an agent's own abilities, as well as its interaction capabilities.

3 Engineering UI from Domain, Context and Task Models

Our process is organized around the components that will be overviewed in this section and described in detailed in Section 4. The different components play different roles; they interact one another by sending the events and transferring the information. Besides, the components use the resources database, mapping rules base [15], layout-knowledge base and so on to achieve their goals. The pro-active and adaptable aspects of the components motivate the adoption the agent paradigm [1] to analyze the models and generate the UI and code. Each component is described as an agent and the various components interact with each other to compose a MAS architecture.

Fig. 1 depicts the main components of our UI and code generation architecture. The *Model analyst* agent uses the *task-*, *database-* knowledge bases and the database itself to analyze the *task* and *domain models* to derive sub-tasks, domain objects and their attributes; the *context model* is also loaded by the *Model analyst* agent. The *Function analyst* agent uses the *Function description* base to define the basic functions of the application. The loaded tasks have to be manually linked to the attributes of the domain objects and to the function defined by the system. From these linked objects, the *UI creator* agent automatically creates the user interface objects based on the *mapping rules*. Once the UI objects have been created, the *code generator* agent generates the code that will implement the UI. Specially, as already pointed out the idea is to not only generate the user interface code, but also the application code behind needed to perform these pre-determined tasks.

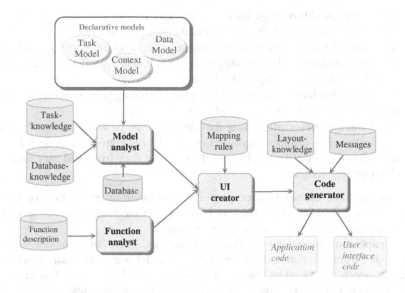

Fig. 1. Main components of user interface generation Architecture

The *model analyst* agent is used to load the task, domain and context models.

In order to obtain the desired behavior of a database application task, the *Function analyst* agent defines the basic functions of an application by using the function description base.

Once the tasks in the task model have been linked to the attributes of the domain objects in the domain model, Concrete Interaction Objects (CIOs) [16] are created based on the attributes characteristics and the relationships between the domain objects by the *UI creator* agent. These characteristics are for instance the data types, data length, is-key flag. Once the CIOs have been created, they are transformed into Final Interaction Objects [16] (FIOs). A FIO is described as a user interface control unit in a concrete platform.

The goal of determining Abstract Interaction Objects [16] (AIOs) is to create CIOs for multi-devices, multi-platforms … This paper focuses on the UI generation for the desktop and laptop devices. Therefore, in our process, the AIOs are not considered.

Finally, the *code generator* agent uses the *Layout-knowledge* base to generate the user interface code based on the FIOs and uses the *Message* base to generate the application code based on the defined functions. The application code is generated to perform the tasks linked to the functions which are defined by the *Function analyst* agent.

In summary, the components of our UI and Code Generation Architecture are:

- The Database used to obtain the information on and of domain model.
- The Task-knowledge base that describes the rules of the task model.
- The Mapping rules base that describes the rules for specifying the CIOs from domain objects and the relationships between these objects and for transforming the CIOs to the FIOs. These rules are described in [15].

- The **Database-knowledge base** that describes generic aspects of the database tasks, the advantages of the syntax and the structure of a query.
- The **Layout-knowledge base** that contains the syntactic design guidelines for controls, windows and other widgets layouts. It also describes the semantic rules from which the control types are defined.
- The **Messages base** that contains the generic messages such as errors, warnings, information to users messages and so on.
- The **Function description base** that describes the basic functions of a database application. For instance, in order to insert the data into a database it has to create a function Insert() which is used to get the data from end user and to input them into the database.

Based on the three classes of user, platforms and environment in the context model [11], we decide to choose the class "user" to support the generation of the user interface. Class user describes the users' characteristics.

This paper aims at reusing the existing resources. The domain model is automatically loaded from a concrete database; the task model is automatically loaded from a XML file which is created by the designer by using the ConcurTaskTreeEnvironment (CTTE) [14] at the analyst level. The user interface is automatically generated based on the links made between the tasks and the attributes of the domain's object. These links are made by the developer.

4   User Interface Generation

This section details the role of the agents and how they communicate with each other to achieve their goals.

4.1   User Interface Generation Social Model

The process proposed in Section 3 is detailed in Fig. 2 using i*. In a few words, i* is an organizational modeling framework [10] proposing concepts such as actor (actors can be agents, positions or roles), as well as social dependencies among actors, including goal, softgoal, task and resource dependencies. Each node represents an actor and each link between two actors indicates a dependency (called dependum) between two actors: the depender and the dependee. The depender is the depending actor, and the dependee, the actor who is depended upon. The type of the dependency may be a goal, a softgoal, a task, or a resource. Goal dependencies represent delegation of responsibility for fulfilling a goal; softgoal dependencies are similar to goal dependencies, but their fulfillment cannot be defined precisely; task dependencies are used in situations where the dependee is required to perform a given activity; and resource dependencies require the dependee to provide a resource to the depender. As partially shown in Fig. 2, actors are represented as circles; dependums (goals, softgoals, tasks and resources) are respectively represented as ovals, clouds, hexagons and rectangles; and dependencies have the form depender → dependum → dependee.

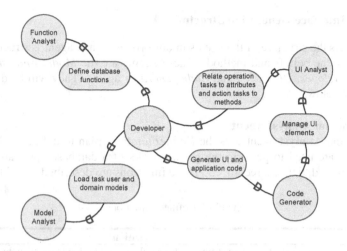

Fig. 2. i* Social Diagram – Processing code generation from task, context and domain models

The ***Developer*** depends on the ***Function Analyst*** agent to define the basic functions of the database application and on the ***Model Analyst*** agent to load the task, user and domain models. The ***UI Analyst*** agent depends on the ***Developer*** to make the links between the tasks and the attributes of the domain's objects. the ***Code Generator*** agent depends on the ***UI Analyst*** to create the UI objects. Finally, the ***Developer*** depends on the ***Code Generator*** agent to generate the user interface code and application code.

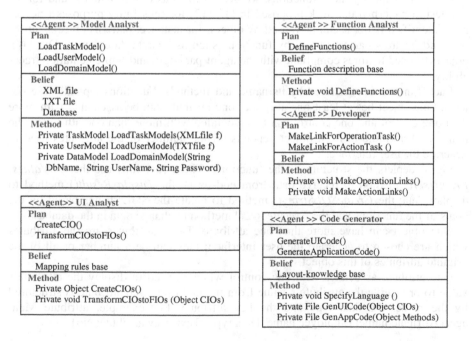

<<Agent >> Model Analyst
Plan
LoadTaskModel()
LoadUserModel()
LoadDomainModel()
Belief
XML file
TXT file
Database
Method
Private TaskModel LoadTaskModels(XMLfile f)
Private UserModel LoadUserModel(TXTfile f)
Private DataModel LoadDomainModel(String
DbName, String UserName, String Password)

<<Agent>> UI Analyst
Plan
CreateCIO()
TransformCIOstoFIOs()
Belief
Mapping rules base
Method
Private Object CreateCIOs()
Private void TransformCIOstoFIOs (Object CIOs)

<<Agent >> Function Analyst
Plan
DefineFunctions()
Belief
Function description base
Method
Private void DefineFunctions()

<<Agent >> Developer
Plan
MakeLinkForOperationTask()
MakeLinkForActionTask ()
Belief
Method
Private void MakeOperationLinks()
Private void MakeActionLinks()

<<Agent >> Code Generator
Plan
GenerateUICode()
GenerateApplicationCode()
Belief
Layout-knowledge base
Method
Private void SpecifyLanguage ()
Private File GenUICode(Object CIOs)
Private File GenAppCode(Object Methods)

Fig. 3. The Agent Structures

4.2   User Interface Generation Structure

Fig. 3 depicts the structure of the agents in our process. Each agent is structured by its name, plans, the beliefs and methods. These agents are the *Model Analyst, Function Analyst, Developer, UI Analyst* and *Code generator* agents. They will be discussed in more detail below.

4.2.1   Function Analyst Agent

The **Function Analyst** agent uses the *DefineFunctions* plan to define the basic functions which are used to perform the generic tasks of a database application such as add a new record, delete a record, …. These functions are described in Table 1.

Table 1. Defined Functions

Function	Description
Display()	Used to select the data stored in the database and to displays this data to the user
AddNew()	Used to insert a data record into the database
Update()	Used to modify the data of an object in the database
Delete()	Used to delete the data records of an object in the database
Search()	Used to filter the data records based on the some search condition which are determined by the user
Review()	Used to review the data records by displaying the first, next, previous and last record

In order to specify these functions, we design them as design patterns and follow the design pattern framework proposed in [13, 12] for reusability purposes (the generic identified patterns can be reused by others, for instance, patterns objects, attributes and controls can be reused by functions such as Search, AddNew or Display), object-oriented features compliant with the agent paradigm and implementation traceability.

Each function is structured by its name and methods. Functions typically use objects. One object has at least one attribute; one attribute can be associated with more than one control and one control can be associated with more than one attribute. The number of attribute of each object depends on the number of the attributes used to generate the user interface.

Fig. 4 depicts the structure of the functions. These functions use the *GetValuesFromUser()* method to receive data from end-users, the *DisplayResult()* method to display data; the *CreateSQLString()* method to create the SQL strings based on the goals of the functions and the *ExecuteSQL()* method to change data in the database.

One object can have more than one attribute. These attributes are the attributes which are chosen to generate the user interface; they can be a number or all of the original attributes of this object.

One attribute associates with one control which is used to display the attribute's value to or receive the attribute's value from the end-user. One attribute is structured by the name, the data type and the key attribute. For example: attribute Manager{Attribute name: Employee name, Data type: Text, Key attribute: No}.

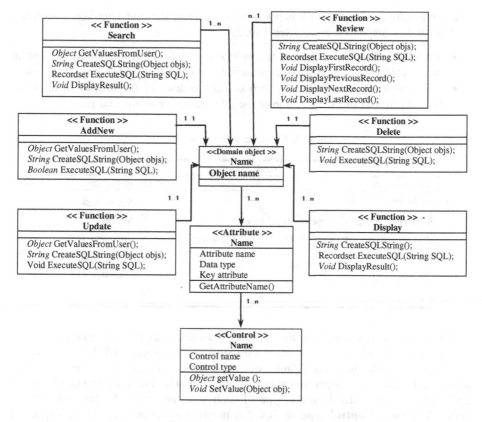

Fig. 4. The Function Structures

One control is structured by the control name, the control type. The getValue() method is used to get data from the end-user and the setValue() is used to display data to the end-user. For example: control Manager{Control name: cbManager, Control type: Combobox}.

In order to obtain the goal, each function has to execute its methods. Each method is executed by the different purposes.

4.2.2 Model Analyst Agent

This agent uses the *LoadTaskModel* plan to load the task model from the XML file, the *LoadDomainModel* to load the domain model from the database and the *LoadUserModel* to load the context model from the TXT file.

The defined categories of tasks at the design level are the action and operation categories. While the categories of tasks, read from the XML file, are abstraction, interaction, cooperation, application and user [13], these categories are defined at the analyst level. At the analyst level, the defined tasks represent different kinds of information including unnecessary ones for UI generation. For instance, the user task is a cognitive task that the end user selects as a strategy to solve a problem or checks the result; typically this type of task is not used to generate the user interface. Therefore, the User task is mapped to none. (See Tab. 2).

- An **Action task** is a task used to describe the end-user command to the system such as close a dialog, search information, open a dialog and so on.
- An **Operation task** is a task which is used to describe the display of information to end-user or the reception of the information from the end-user.

Table 2. Tasks are mapped as follows

Task mapping	
Analyst level	Design level
Abstraction task	Action task
Interaction task (Type: Control type)	Action
Interaction task (Type: Edit\Monitoring\ selection)	Operation task
Cooperation task	Action task
Application task	Operation task
User task	None

Fig. 5 depicts an example of the mapping between tasks in ConcurTaskTrees and in our process considering a typical AccessStudent Data task. Task *Verify* is not focused; task *AccesstudentData* is automatically mapped to action task; task ShowResults is automatically mapped to operation task; and other tasks are mapped to action and operation tasks based on the type of each task. For example: the task type of *SubmitRequest* is **Control type** so that it is mapped to action task; the task types of *EnterName* and *EnterDepartment* are **Edit** and **Selection** then they are mapped to operation tasks.

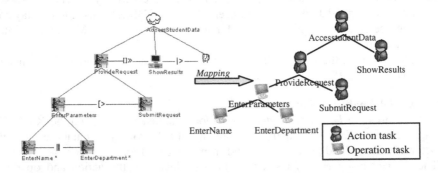

Fig. 5. Example of Mapping: an AccessStudentData task.

The *LoadUserModel* plan is used to analyze the information in the user model to classify the users into three different classes base on their ability to use the software. The analyzed information is the characteristics of the users such as the experience, skill, knowledge, behavior so on. The three classes of the user model are named "Simple",

"Mean" and "Complex" corresponding to three ability levels for using the software. Based on these user classes, the designer will design a complex, medium or simple user interface.

Finally, the *LoadDomainModel* plan is used to load the domain model from a concrete database which is determined by the developer. The *LoadDomainModel* plan executes the SQL queries to obtain the information of the domain objects (table names), their attributes (column names), aspects of these attributes (column attributes) and relationships between these objects.

4.2.3 Developer

The **Developer** uses the *MakeLinkForOperationTask* and the *MakeLinkForAction-Task* plans to make the links between task model and domain model. The *Make-LinkForOperationTask* plan is used to make the associations between leaf operation tasks and attributes of domain's objects. All of the leaf operation task has to be linked to at least one attribute of the domain's. The *MakeLinkForActionTask* plan is used to make the links between the action tasks and the defined functions. One action task is linked to only one defined function (Search Employee task in the Fig. 6). The action tasks not linked to the defined function are linked to default function (Exit task in the Fig. 6).

As depicted in the Fig. 6, one operation task can be linked to more than one attribute of domain's object and one attribute of domain's object can be linked to more than one operation task.

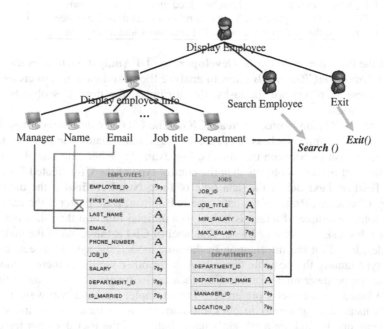

Fig. 6. Making the links between the tasks and the attributes of domain's objects, defined functions

4.2.4 UI Analyst Agent

There are two important UI objects are used in our process. These objects are Concrete Interaction Object and Final Interface Object.

A *Concrete Interaction Object* (CIO) is a graphical object for entering and displaying the data that the user can see, feel and manipulate [15]. A CIO is synonymous to a control, a physical interactor, a widget or a presentation object such as text-field, combo-box, check-box, button … A CIO in our process is defined by its label, control type, editable attributes as follows:

Concrete Interaction Object
Label: The label of the CIO; it will be used to label the control
Control type: The control type which is used to communicate between the user and computer's system
Editable: *Yes* if this control can be edited by end-user; otherwise *No*

The **Final Interface Object** (FIO) represents the operational interface object that is running on a special computing platform either by interpretation (e.g., through a web browser) or by execution. The FIO is determined based on the CIO in a certain language, on a certain platform and so on. A FIO defined as follows:

Final Interaction Object
Label: The label of the control
Control type: The control type is specified in certain platform
Editable: *Yes* if this control can be edited by end-user; otherwise *No*
Position: The position (X, Y) of control in a form or in the screen
Size: The dimension of the control, it contains width and height

Since the links are made by the **Developer**, the **UI Analyst** agent uses the *CreateCIO* and *TransformCIOstoFIOs* plans to analyze the linked elements to create the UI objects. These elements are the tasks, the attributes, the domain's objects and the defined functions.

The *CreateCIO* plan is used to create CIOs. The CIOs are determined based on the features of the attribute such as data type (Text/Number/Date), the primary key, ect and the relationships between the objects. For example: When one task derives from the attributes of domain's objects then the control type of the CIO created for this task is **Text field** or **Text box** if the data type is Text; **Number field** if the data type is Number; **Check box/Radio** if the data type is Boolean; Date picker if the data type is Date. Another example, if a task is linked to a defined function then the control type of CIO of this task is Button or Menu. The label of CIO is the name of the task.

Besides, based on the information in the user model, the system selects a correct control type among the possible control types. In other words, if there is more than one control type determined for one CIO then our software chooses one of them for this CIO based on the user's preference. For example: we have two ways to open a student's name dialog; one is to click on students menu then choose the student's name menu, one is click on a student's name button. If the user does not have computer experience it is better if the UI is a button. He/She cans understand exactly, quickly what he/she needs to act to open a dialog to see the student's name.

The *TransformCIOstoFIOs* plan is used to transform the CIOs to FIOs. The FIOs are specified based on the attributes of the CIOs and the programming language determined by the developer. For each CIO, a correlative concrete control is created. As discussed, a CIO is defined by the attributes *Name, control type, editable, position* and *size*.

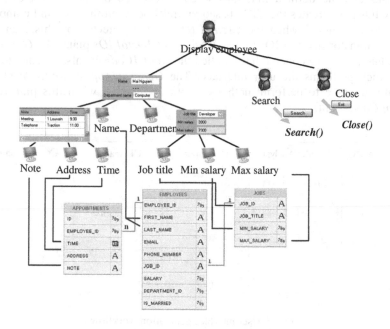

Fig. 7. An example for creating the FIOs

Fig. 7 depicts how the FOIs are created based on the links between the tasks and the attributes, the features of the attributes of domain model and the relationships between the domain's object.

4.2.5 Code Generator Agent

The **Code Generator** agent uses the *SpecifyLanguage* plan to specify the language used to perform the user interface determined above, the *GenerateUICode* plan to generate the code based on the determined FIOs and the *GenerateApplicationCode* to perform the function determined in the *FunctionAnalyst* agent.

4.3 User Interface Generation Workflow

Fig. 8 models the plan diagram depicting the control flow from the Function Analyst agent defining the basic functions to the Code Generator agent creating the user interface. We summarize below some specific points of the generation workflow depicting the relationships between plans and events.

Once the *DefineFunction* plan defines the functions, it sends the *loadModel* event to the *LoadTaskModel, LoadUserModel* and *LoadDomainModel* plans to load task, user and domain models. The *MakeLinkForOperationTask* plan makes links between the operation tasks and the attributes of domain's objects when it received the LinkOTask event. The *MakeLinkForActionTask* plan makes links between the action tasks and the defined functions when it received the *LinkATask* event. The CreateCIOs plan creates the CIOs based on links between the task and components of the domain model when the *CreateCIO* event is detected by this plan. These CIOs are transformed to FIOs by the *TransformCIOstoFIOs* plan. The *GenerateUI-Code* plan is triggered once it has handled the *GenUICode* events to generate the UI code which performs the user interface. The *GenerateApplicationCode* plan will generate the code to perform methods of our application when this plan receives *GenAppCode* event.

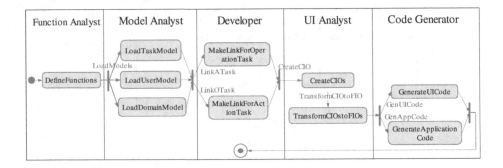

Fig. 8. User interface generation workflow

Since the tasks are associated with the attributes of the domain's objects and the defined functions, the user interface is automatically generated based on the features of the attributes and the relationships between the domain's objects.

5   Code Generator

The Code Generator is made to help developer to easily create the user interface from the task, user and domain models. Especially, Code Generator also automatically generates the application code for performing the defined functions which are discussed in the section 4.2.1. The task model is load from a XML file which is made by designer by using the CTTE [14]. The domain model is load from a concrete database which is determined by the developer. And finally, the user model is load from a text file.

As depicted in the Fig. 9, once the developer chooses a task from the list of tasks then the sub-tasks of this task is displayed in the left of screen. The sub-task are displayed are all of the sub-tasks at level 1 and all of the *operation* tasks at other levels. The domain's objects are displayed in the right of the screen. The UI objects are described in the table in the bottom of the screen.

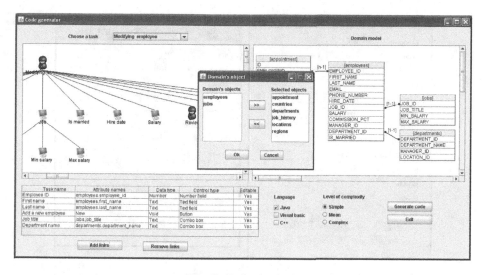

Fig. 9. Code generator

Fig. 10. Associating operation task *Employee name* to attributes First_Name, Last_Name and action task *Review Employees* to Review() function

The link between a leaf operation task and the attributes of the domain's objects is made by focusing the task and selecting the relevant attributes then putting on "Add link" button. The link between a leaf action task and a defined function is made by focusing the task and selecting the relevant function from a list of functions. Each action task is linked to only one function and each function is linked to only one task. (See Fig. 10).

The links are removed by selecting these links in the table then putting on "Remove links" button.

The generated code is generated when the developer puts on the "Generate code" button. The generated code can be compiled and ran immediately. The forms in the Fig. 11 are the result of the using the Code Generator. The selected language in this case is java. Beside generating the UI code, the code generator also generates the application code automatically for creating, deleting, reviewing the information of the employees.

The generated user interface is not useful as the user interface generated in a traditional manner are for the following reasons:

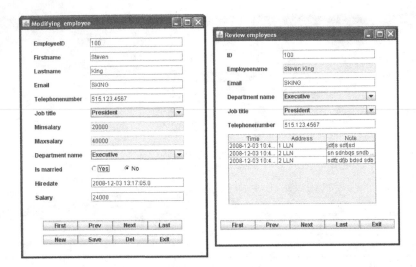

Fig. 11. Forms generated

- The controls are automatically designed in the order of creating the links between components of the task and domain models. They are not arranged reasonably.
- In the case of selecting alternative solutions, a traditional manner works better than an automatic manner since the developer can decide the best solution with his experience, knowledge, domain ...

6 Conclusions

To be efficient, data-intensive systems that are an important component of today's software applications need effective human-computer interaction. User interfaces for such data systems has been a recurrent research issue and nowadays these UI have to support automatic generation to adequately be dealt with.

We have proposed here a framework whose purpose is to drive the automatic database user interface design and code behind generation from the task, user and domain model combined together.

This framework has aimed at offering a low cost, short time-to-implementation and efficient development environment from the business user side. Indeed, the objective is not to provide a tool for supporting the development of the database applications to not only the developers but also to support non-IT end-user. Because this tool is easy to use and the generated code cans run immediately.

References

1. Do, T.: A framework for multi-agent systems detailed desgn. Ph.D. Thesis, Université Catholique de Louvain, Institut d'Administration et de Gestion (IAG), Louvain La Neuve, Belgique (July 2005)

2. Julien, D., Ziane, M., Guessoum, Z.: GOLIATH: An extensible model-based environment to develop user interfaces. In: Proceedings of the Fourth International Conference on Computer Aided Design for User Interfaces (2004)

3. Da Silva, P.P., Griffiths, T., Paton, N.: Generating user interface code in a model based user interface development environment. In: Proc. of Advanced Visual Interfaces (AVI 2000), New York, pp. 155–160 (2000)

4. Mahfoudhi, A., Abed, M., Abid, M.: Towards a User Interface Generation Approach Based on Object Oriented Design and Task Model. In: TAMODIA 2005: 4th International Workshop on TAsk MOdels and DIAgrams for user interface design For Work and Beyond Gdansk, Poland, September 26-27 (2005)

5. Rosado da Cruz, A.M., Pascoal de Faria, J.: Automatic Generation of User Interfaces from Domain and Use Case Models. In: Quality of Information and Communications Technology, QUATIC 2007, pp. 208–212 (2007)

6. Zambonelli, F., Jennings, N.R., Wooldridge, M.: Organizational abstractions for the analysis and design of multi-agent systems. In: Ciancarini, P., Wooldridge, M.J. (eds.) AOSE 2000. LNCS, vol. 1957, pp. 235–251. Springer, Heidelberg (2001)

7. Pribeanu, C.: Tool Support for Handling Mapping Rules from Domain to Task Models. In: Coninx, K., Luyten, K., Schneider, K.A. (eds.) TAMODIA 2006. LNCS, vol. 4385, pp. 16–23. Springer, Heidelberg (2007)

8. Wooldridge, M., Jennings, N.R.: Intelligent agents: Theory and practice. The Knowledge Engineering Review 10(2), 115–152 (1995)

9. Wooldridge, M., Jennings, N.R.: Special Issue on Intelligent Agents and Multi-Agent Systems. Applied Artificial Intelligence Journal 9(4), 74–86 (1996)

10. Yu, E.: Modelling Strategic Relationships for Process Reengineering. Ph.D Thesis, Dept of Computer Science, University of Toronto, Canada (1995)

11. Calvary, G., Coutaz, J., Thevenin, D., Limbourg, Q., Bouillon, L., Vander-donckt, J.: A Unifying Reference Framework for Multi-Target User Interfaces. Interacting with Computers 15(3), 289–308 (2003)

12. Forbrig, P., Lämmel, R.: Programming with Patterns. In: Proceedings TOOLS-USA 2000. IEEE, Los Alamitos (2000)

13. Gamma, E., Helm, R., Johnson, R., Vlissides, J.: Patterns: Elements of Reusable Object-Oriented Software. Addison-Wesley, Reading (1994)

14. Paternò, F., Mori, G., Galiberti, R.: CTTE: an environment for analysis and development of task models of cooperative applications. In: CHI 2001 Extended Abstracts on Human Factors in Computer Systems, Seattle, pp. 21–22. ACM Press, New York (2001)

15. Tran, V., Vanderdonckt, J., Kolp, M., Faulkner, S.: Generating User Interface from Task, User and Domain Models. In: Proceedings of the Second International Conference on Advances in Human-oriented and Personalized Mechanisms, Technologies, and Services, Centric 2009 (2009)

16. Vanderdonckt, J., Bodart, F.: Encapsulating Knowledge for Intelligent Automatic Interaction Objects Selection. In: Proc. of the ACM Conf. on Human Factors in Computing Systems INTERCHI 1993, Amsterdam, April 24-29, pp. 424–429. ACM Press, New York (1993)

Author Index